JACK LONDON

American Rebel

Philip S. Foner

THE CITADEL PRESS · New York

Preface

Jack London: American Rebel was originally published in 1947. It consisted of a collection of his social writings and a study of the man and his times. In the preface to that volume, I wrote that all over Europe and Asia and in outlying parts of the world thousands of copies of London's social writings still circulated annually. "Yet in his own country the social writings of Jack London have been permitted to lie buried. Search the vast majority of American book stores and libraries, and one will find only a stray copy here and there. . . ."

In reissuing *Jack London: American Rebel*, I have decided to omit the selections from his social writings and publish only the study of the man as a social critic in thought and action. The social writings which made up a large part of *Jack London: American Rebel* can now be found in many libraries.

In the original preface I wrote the following, which is worth repeating, though I would add the name Mark Twain to the list of London's literary predecessors:

"Upton Sinclair spoke the truth when he said that Jack London's social writings 'constitute him one of the great revolutionary figures in our history.' These writings occupy an important place in the long American tradition of protest and revolt, a tradition associated with the names of other American rebels—Jefferson and Paine, Emerson and Thoreau, Whittier and Whitman. It is true that the oft-cited contradictions in Jack London produced decided flaws in his social philosophy and ultimately weakened his attachment to the main source of strength in American life, the people themselves. But in spite of these shortcomings, Jack London was one of the outstanding interpreters and champions of the American socialist movement prior to the First World War. In the biographical study which accompanies this collection of London's social writings, I have sought to relate in detail his unique contributions to this movement. I concern myself chiefly with those aspects of his life and writings in which he played the role of a social rebel. Other aspects of his life and work have been dealt with in various studies, whereas this side of his career has been comparatively neglected."

There is little that has appeared since 1947 that requires any alteration in the original text of this biographical study. I have, however, added a section at the close of the biography which did not appear in the original edition. This section consists mainly of additional material from letters of London or interviews with him in the contemporary press for which there was no room in the original edition. There are also some extracts from London's writings which were not included in that edition. Finally, there are a few comments by other students of Jack London and some additional information which has come to light since 1947. All of this material is indicated by references to the page and line of the particular item in the biography to which they refer.

PHILIP S. FONER

Croton-on-Hudson, New York
December 1, 1963

Contents

Jack London: American Rebel

"No American writer," said Fred Lewis Pattee of Jack London, "has had a career more representative of his time." To this one should add that no American writer was a more articulate and splendid spokesman for his time. For it was Jack London more than any other writer of his day, who broke the ice that was congealing American letters and brought life and literature into a meaningful relation to each other.

The end of the nineteenth century found the nation in a state of great social and political unrest. It found expression in the rise of the labor movement, furious battles between labor and capital, and the political conflict between farmers, workers and small business men on the one hand and the powerful monopolies on the other. Yet throughout this turbulent period there was a curious dichotomy between literature and life. Anyone dependent upon American letters to guide him would have obtained the most confused and inaccurate conceptions of the life led by more than sixty millions of Americans and of the major problems confronting them. He would find that the American people were concerned solely with romantic love sometimes enacted in remote times by men and women in costume who addressed each other as "thee" and "thou," or in imagined principalities of Europe like Zenda or Graustark where gilt-uniformed officers wooed beautiful heroines on marbled terraces. If the romance was set in contemporary America it was all in the fragrance of new-mown hay or of magnolias surrounding white-columned verandas. The teeming life of the industrial city produced the formula of the poor boy who married the boss's daughter and was taken into the firm.

Of the grinding poverty of the workers, of wretched housing, low wages, long hours and unsanitary working conditions, of child labor, of the ruthless industrial and financial tycoons, the literature of the day said little. By an almost universal agreement among editors and publishers they were considered unmentionable and unfit for literary presentation. Theodore Dreiser, recalling his early days as a journalist in New York, has recorded in *A Book About Myself* his reactions to the failure of contemporary literature to deal faithfully with American life:

> *In a kind of ferment or fever due to my necessities and desperation, I set to examining the current magazines and fiction and articles to be found therein*—Century, Scribner's, Harper's. *I was never more confounded than by the discrepancy existing between my own observations and those displayed here, the beauty and peace and charm to be found in everything, the complete absence of any reference to the coarse and the cruel and the terrible. How did it happen that these remarkable persons, geniuses of course, one and all, saw life in this happy roseate? Was it so and was I all wrong? . . . They seemed to deal with phases of sweetness and beauty and success and goodness such as I rarely encountered. . . .*
>
> *When I think of the literary and social snobbery and bosh of that day, its utter futility and profound faith in its own goodness, as opposed to facts of its own visible life, I have to smile.*

Beginning with Rebecca Harding Davis' "Life in the Iron Mills" in *The Atlantic* of April, 1861, probably the earliest treatment of the lives of industrial workers that approached realism, American fiction since the Civil War had occasionally piped a rather feeble note of social criticism. Elizabeth Stuart Phelps' *The Silent Partner*, Edward Bellamy's *Looking Backward*, and William Dean Howells' *A Traveler from Altruria*, were among the books published before 1890 which attempted to get close to real life in America. But these were drowned in the avalanche of fiction which depicted only the pleasant side of life, and shied away from the harsh, the sordid, the real. Even Howells himself wrote that "the more smiling aspects of life are the more American."

Here and there a few Americans attempted to introduce Tolstoy, Zola, Turgeniev, Flaubert, Ibsen, Sudermann, Hauptmann and other

European realists to the American reading public and to recommend their methods to American writers. But they came against the stone wall of editorial opposition which insisted that American authors repeat the time-worn formulas of the pseudo-romance. Realism was condemned as indecent; literature must be "suited to maiden ears and eyes," and there must be an end to the "disposition which may well be called alarming, to trifle with the marriage relation." It was not art but contented itself "with photographing the transitory surfaces of life." It was pessimistic, depressing, and degrading, and no writer had "a right to make this beautiful, puzzling, sad world any more mournful than it is for everybody else." Most important of all, it was critical of contemporary society and filled with revolutionary ideas. "All this hacking at wealth," cried Maurice Thompson, a leading champion of the romantic school of literature, "and all this apostrophizing of poverty is not the spirit of Christ; it is in the spirit of communism, socialism and anarchy. . . ."

Upon this scene there stepped several young writers who at the turn of the century blazed new trails in American literature. Influenced by the European naturalistic and realistic tradition, and conscious of the growing class conflicts in their own country, they resolved to introduce into the thin, pale, bloodless, sentimental, insipid writing of the day, themes, characters and styles which were reflections of American life itself. At the same time, new and daring figures, like Frank A. Munsey, John Brisbane Walker and S. S. McClure, entered the magazine field. Aware of the startling technological advances which were reducing the cost of publishing, these men began to think in terms of huge circulation at low prices to a mass audience as yet untapped. To attract and hold this new audience these men vied with each other in publishing vital literature, replete with meaning for the times. *Munsey's, McClure's* and *Cosmopolitan* at ten cents a copy made the older magazines, purveying tranquil fiction and sedate essays to an exclusive public and selling for twenty-five and thirty-five cents, appear uninspired. Furthermore, the stronger organization of labor and the growth of the socialist movement brought into being a chain of radical periodicals, *The Appeal to Reason, The Comrade, Wilshire's Magazine,* the *International Socialist Review,* which offered a medium for material which was too strong even for the popular magazines and which formed a rallying point for a new school of American writers.

This new trend in American literature made its debut with the

6   JACK LONDON

publication at the author's expense of Stephen Crane's *Maggie: A Girl of the Streets* in 1893. Six years later, Frank Norris, a devoted disciple of Emile Zola, laid the plans for his "Epic of Wheat" which in three novels would tell the story "of this huge Niagara of wheat," from its growth and harvesting in the West, through the speculation in the Chicago Wheat Pit, to its mission of feeding India's starving millions during a famine. Only two of the books, *The Octopus* and *The Pit,* were completed, for Norris died before he could start the third.

Crane and Norris were the pioneers of realism in modern American literature, but their writings did not reflect the most important issue confronting the American people in their day—the furious battle between labor and capital. Nor were they interested chiefly in protesting economic evils in society. In dedicating a copy of *Maggie* to a Baptist minister, Crane wrote: "It tries to show that environment is a tremendous thing in this world, and often shapes lives regardlessly. If I could prove that theory I would make room in heaven for all sorts of souls (notably an occasional street girl) who are not confidently expected to be there by many excellent people." But with the efforts of the working class to change their environment and to make room for a better society on earth, Crane was not concerned. Even Norris, for all his compassion and sense of justice, did not write to mobilize the people in the battle against economic injustice. Evils existed in society, to be sure, but they were subordinate to the all-prevailing, inevitable goodness of nature. Thus he wrote in the final paragraph of his greatest novel, *The Octopus,* the story of a futile uprising of San Joaquin Valley farmers against the Southern Pacific Railroad:

> *Falseness dies; injustice and oppression in the end of everything fade and vanish away. Greed, cruelty, selfishness and inhumanity are short-lived; the individual suffers, but the race goes on. Annixter dies, but in a far-distant corner of the world a thousand lives are saved. The larger view always and through all shams, all wickedness, discovers the Truth that will, in the end, prevail, and all things, surely, inevitably, resistlessly, work together for good.*

But another American writer was emerging who was interested not only in exposing cruelties and oppressions in the economic system, but in remaking it and building a new and better social order. This was Jack London. Like Crane and Norris he was a realist, but unlike

them he was also a socialist, and from his belief in Marxism as a philosophy of history he drew the ability to describe, better than any of
his predecessors or his contemporaries and most of those who followed him, the modern social struggle out of which would inevitably
come the regeneration of mankind. London was not the equal of
Crane or Norris in literary finish nor in balanced characterization;
his style was often melodramatic and his writing was frequently
marred by flaws of structure, but it achieved stature by its sheer in-
tensity of conviction and its great love for the working people and
their aspirations. London knew the life of which he wrote; knew how
workers lived and talked and how to transfer the details of their lives
to the printed page with amazing fidelity. And the workers read this
writing, reread it and passed it along until the pages were shredded.
In the January, 1929 issue of the *New Masses*, Martin Russak wrote:

> *A real proletarian writer must not only write about the
> working class, he must be read by the working class. A real
> proletarian writer must not only use his proletarian life as
> material; his writing must burn with the spirit of revolt. Jack
> London was a real proletarian writer—the first and so far the
> only proletarian writer of genius in America. Workers who
> read, read Jack London. He is the one author they have all
> read, he is one literary experience they all have in common.
> Factory workers, farm hands, seamen, miners, newsboys read
> him and read him again. He is the most popular writer of the
> American working class.*

Before Jack London, the fiction dealing with the working class was
characterized by sympathy for labor and the underprivileged, but
chiefly in the spirit of Christian principles of brotherhood, proclaiming as its message that if only labor and capital could be persuaded
to follow the teachings of Christ, all social and economic problems
could be solved. Most of these writers were convinced that injustices
existed in our economic system, and against these injustices they
protested, but they had no wish to change the system itself; or if they
did, through idealistic, utopian schemes. For the most part, too, these
writers were not workers themselves writing of their own experiences.
They wrote about the working class as interested but objective ob-
servers, hoping as humanitarians to improve the living conditions of
labor without shaking the economic structure. Frequently they discussed trade unions and strikes, but only to prove that force of any

kind brought disaster upon the workers. Most of this writing ended with a sentimental plea to soften the hearts of the capitalists and infuse them with a belated spirit of brotherly love.

Life itself led Jack London to reject this approach in his writing. As a newsboy, sailor, mill-hand, stoker, tramp, and janitor, he came to know all there was to know about the life of the underdog. He knew what it meant to be one of the disinherited, to be chained to the deadening routine of the machine and to soul-destroying labor for an insufficient reward. Consequently he swept aside not only the literature that pretended that ours is a society of sweetness and light, but also that which contended that the inculcation of the spirit of Christian fellowship would put an end to class controversy. He did not oppose labor organization nor balk at the strike as a weapon of labor; rather, he took his heroes and heroines from the labor movement and wove his plots within their struggles. His own proletarian background had taught him that the individual worker was powerless in the face of the greed of the ruling class. He was not content to appeal for the end of poverty and ignorance and disease; he called for the destruction of the system which was responsible for these evils. He poured into his writings all the pain of his life, the fierce hatred of the bourgeoisie that it had produced in him, and the conviction it had brought to him that the world could be made a better place to live in if the exploited would rise up and take the management of society out of the hands of the exploiters. Even after he had established his fame and money-making power in the popular magazines, he did not forget his proletarian origins. He risked the rewards of his years of labor on the road up from poverty and obscurity to write socialist essays and revolutionary stories and novels. He became the most successful writer of his day, but he remained the most radical writer in American literature.

Jack London was born in San Francisco, California on January 12, 1876, the son of William Henry Chaney, an itinerant astrologer and Flora Wellman, a spiritualist. When he was eight months old, his mother married John London, a migrant worker and farmer, and took her young son to the London flat in the working-class section south of Market Street. From his foster-father Jack Chaney took the name by which he is known to history.

When Jack London came into the world it was in the midst of the crisis which began in September, 1873 when the banking house of

Jay Cook and Company closed its doors. By the time he was a year old hundreds of thousands of workers were jobless and the employed were forced to submit to reduction of wages ranging from forty to sixty per cent. All over the country homeless workers, the tramps of the 'seventies, wandered about picking up odd jobs when they were fortunate, but mainly living in shacks and gleaning the garbage heaps for food. In San Francisco, communities of homeless workers dotted the outskirts of the city living on food "that a humane man would hesitate about throwing to his dog."

The depression did not leave the London family untouched. During the first five years of Jack's childhood the family moved about constantly while John London tried his hand at various occupations. At times they were fairly well off, but they never knew security. And the constant moving about—the family changed its residence five times in as many years—provided additional hardships for the youngster. Each time the family moved, Jack had to make new friends, and very often during his childhood he was to know what it meant to have no playmates.

In 1880 the family, penniless after an unsuccessful grocery store venture, tried its hand at raising corn and other vegetables on a twenty-acre farm in Alameda. From there they moved to a desolate ranch in San Mateo where they were to remain for the next three years, in hardships that dwarfed anything they had hitherto experienced. London calls this the hungriest period in his life. So hungry was he that at one time he stole a tiny piece of meat from a girl's lunch-basket. It was with the greatest effort that he stopped himself from retrieving the unwanted scraps of meat that his schoolmates threw to the ground. Years later he wrote of this period in his life:

> *I had been poor. Poor I had lived. I had gone hungry on occasion. I had never had toys nor playthings like other children. My first memories of life were pinched by poverty. The pinch of poverty had become chronic. . . . And only a child, with a child's imagination, can come to know the meaning of things it has long been denied.*

When Jack was eight, the family moved to Livermore Valley. Here he discovered "the authentic passion of his life," the love of books. His teacher loaned him Washington Irving's *The Alhambra*. He scoured the homes of his neighbors and came upon Paul du Chaillu's

Explorations and Adventures in Equatorial Africa and Ouida's *Signa,* the romantic story of an Italian peasant lad who rose to fame as a composer. He read everything and anything he could lay his hands on, although most of his literary fare consisted of dime novels and old newspaper serials featuring the adventures of "poor but virtuous shopgirls." Next year when the family moved back to Oakland, he made the acquaintance of the Oakland Public Library and every moment he could spare found him buried in a book. He read all the time, at meals, after meals, on the way to and from school and during recess. If hunger had not interfered, he would have sat with his books all day long "and read, and read, and read, and read."

But John London was once again out of work, and it was up to Jack to furnish food for the poverty-stricken family. He awoke at 3 A.M. to deliver newspapers, after which he went on to school. After school hours he delivered the evening papers. Week-ends he worked on an ice wagon, in a bowling alley, and as a porter. All of his earnings he turned over to his family.

What time he could spare from his work, from school and from his reading, he spent at the water-front seeking an escape from the humdrum of his life. By scraping together nickels and dimes he managed to accumulate enough money to buy an old boat first and later a second-hand skiff. Every spare moment found him in the saloons supplementing his formal education by what he learned from the water front characters, or taking ever longer sails on the treacherous San Francisco Bay.

When he was graduated, at the age of thirteen, from the Oakland grammar school, he was named class historian, and chosen to deliver a speech at the graduation exercises. But his clothes were too ragged for the acceptance of honors, and Jack did not even show up formally to receive his diploma. The financial situation in the London household put high school out of the question, for Jack's earnings were now urgently needed to supplement the family income. For a year he continued selling papers morning and night, plus whatever odd jobs he could pick up. Then his foster-father was struck by a train and seriously hurt. The family moved again, this time to a broken down cottage on the Estuary surrounded by shacks built of driftwood.

He found work in a cannery in West Oakland. His pay—ten cents an hour—was so low that even a ten-hour shift did not net him enough for the family's pressing needs. So he worked overtime, standing at the same machine for eighteen and twenty hours at a stretch. Once he worked for thirty-six consecutive hours, after which, as was his custom, he walked home, unable to spare the money for carfare.

For several months he continued the back-breaking routine—up in the morning at half-past five, at the machine until after dark, home from work, numb with fatigue and in bed after midnight. And then both his mind and body rebelled. The vision of being tied to the machine for the rest of his life and gradually sapped of all vitality and ambition horrified him and he sought escape. His life on the water front had made him familiar with the ways of the oyster pirates who raided the beds owned by a few companies in Lower Bay and sold their loot for high prices on the Oakland docks. A man who owned his own boat, he knew, could make as much in one night as he brought home in several months' work at the cannery. And instead of the monotonous work at the machine he would be out on a boat in the company of hard-fisted, hard-drinking men. At one stroke, his financial problems would be solved and his love of adventure satisfied.

So Jack London, not yet fifteen, borrowed $300 from Mammy Jenny, his Negro wet-nurse, and bought the *Razzle-Dazzle*, a fast sloop owned by French Frank, one of the older pirates. The next night Jack made his first raid on the oyster-beds. French's sixteen-year-old girl-friend, Mame, queen of the oyster pirates, and eighteen other water front characters with names like Spider, Big George, Young Scratch Nelson, Whiskey Bob, and Nicky the Greek made up the crew. The following morning he was back in Oakland selling the loot. In one night he had made three months' cannery wages. Within a short time he paid Mammy Jenny back her loan.

For a year or more he sailed San Francisco Bay, robbing oyster-beds, living recklessly and, between raids, reading books borrowed from the public library. Any night he might receive a bullet through his head from the rifles of the Fish Patrol or a knife in his back from the hand of some drunken member of his crew. But to Jack all this was secondary to the new-found adventure and the ability to make money easily. Within six months he became known as the Prince of the Oyster Pirates. A little while later he added the title, Prince of the Drunkards. He got drunk on raw whiskey whenever he was not on raids, and although he made as much as $180 in a night's raid, he was constantly broke. He no longer contributed to his family; the saloons received the money which should have gone for food and rent. The water front gave the fifteen-year-old "Prince" no more than a year to live!

Along the Oakland water front [writes F. L. Pattee] *the old salts will even now be recounting ripping tales of the young "daredevil London," who could drink any man down at the bar, and knock any two of them down at once, who had the temerity to refuse his invitation to "line-up."*

Jack might have been able to forget his sordid childhood and wretched boyhood in drink. But raw whiskey almost ended his career at fifteen. One morning at 1 A.M. he accidentally fell into the water. He had been drinking for three weeks continuously. A fit of despondency seized him and he decided to drown himself. All night long he swam and floated in the bay, waiting for exhaustion to carry him under. But, sobered by the cold water, he changed his mind. This was no solution to his problems. He struck out across the current, and daylight found him, completely exhausted, fighting the tides off Mare Island. A few minutes more and all would have been over. Fortunately, a Greek fisherman hauled him in, unconscious.

A few days after the rescue, while running in a load of oysters, Jack was hailed by a State officer and offered an opportunity to become a deputy for the Fish Patrol to police the same waters he had so skilfully pillaged. The pay was fifty per cent of the fines collected. Jack accepted and soon experienced the same joy in sailing the waters of the Bay as a Patrol officer that he had known as a pirate.

He worked for the Fish Patrol for almost a year. But the more he had to do with it the more disgusted he became with the politicians who controlled it. It sickened him to discover that the officials were crooked and venal and not men who received their offices through ability and public service.

His disillusionment quickened his desire for a change. In January, 1893, Jack shipped out aboard the *Sophie Sutherland* headed for Korea, Japan and Siberia. On board ship he used his fists to win acceptance as an equal by the hard-bitten seamen who regarded boys as door mats to be stepped upon and slaves to cater to their whims. He had signed on as an able-bodied seaman, and though he knew enough to cover himself, he also understood the resentment of the older men who had gone through all the hard knocks of life to gain a similar rating. He won them over with his wit, his fists and his daring exploits. One night, when drunk, he swam all alone through the ink-black harbor of Yokohama, a feat which almost cost him his life but established him in the eyes of the older men.

Seven months at sea were enough. He returned to San Francisco, stopped to buy a round of drinks for former friends, bought a second-hand hat, coat and vest, a few shirts and two suits of underclothes, and went directly to Oakland. There he found the family on the verge of starvation. Jack paid the bills and turned the rest of his savings over to his mother. Then he set out to look for a job.

But while Jack London had been hunting seals off the Siberian coast, drinking and listening to the yarns of sealers and sailors, and, after a sufficient number of whiskeys, brawling with the natives, the severest economic crisis America had yet experienced swept the nation. By the time he returned to Oakland the panic of 1893 had paralyzed the industrial structure, knocked the bottom under wages, and reduced to idleness three million workers. He saw jobless men everywhere, wandering through the city in search of work, only to be joined by workers being discharged from the places where they applied. He saw thousands standing in line all night waiting for work at ten cents an hour.

The only work Jack could find was in a jute mill where for ten hours of back-breaking labor he earned one dollar. At his side were children, some eight years of age, earning a little over thirty cents for the same working day. He stayed on for several months, hoping each week to receive the dollar and a quarter a day the owners of the mill had promised him.

After a day spent in the mill Jack was in no condition to think of anything besides getting to bed. Yet it was under such conditions that he published his first story. Years later he told reporters how he got his start as a writer:

> *In my fitful school days I had written the usual composition which had been praised in the usual way, and while working in the jute mills I still made an occasional try. The factory occupied thirteen hours of my day, and being young and husky, I wanted a little for myself, so there was not much left for composition. The* San Francisco Call *offered a prize for a descriptive article. My mother urged me to try for it, and I did, taking for my subject, "Typhoon off the Coast of China."*
>
> *Very tired and sleepy and knowing I had to be up at 5:30, I began the article at midnight and worked straight on until I had written 2,000 words, the limit of the article, but with my idea only half worked out. I continued, adding another 2,000*

> *words before I had finished, and the third night I spent in*
> *cutting out the excess, so as to bring the article within the*
> *conditions of the contest. The first prize came to me, and my*
> *success seriously turned my thoughts to writing, but my blood*
> *was still too hot for a settled routine.*

On November 12, 1893, the *San Francisco Call* announced that the five judges had unanimously awarded the twenty-five dollars first prize to "Story of a Typhoon off the Coast of Japan, by John London aged 17—address—1321 Twenty-second Avenue, Oakland."

After another effort at a sea tale brought no response from the *Call,* Jack resigned himself to his job at the jute mill. But not for long. The promised raise did not materialize, and he realized he was rapidly getting nowhere. He quit, deciding to learn a trade. Trade school was out of the question, for he had to earn money to support the family. The next best thing was to get into some industry, start at the bottom and work himself up. He hit upon the field of electricity, which was just making its influence felt in American industry.

When Jack applied for a job at the power plant of the Oakland Street Railway, he was overjoyed to discover that the superintendent sympathized with young men who were not afraid of hard work and were willing to do anything to get a start. He gave Jack the job of feeding coal to the enormous furnaces, assuring him that in time he would become an oiler, an assistant to the mechanics, and eventually, depending, of course, on himself, he might go clear to the top. Jack added the rest himself—promotion after promotion and finally the hand of the boss's daughter in marriage. Later he wrote of himself: "I formulated a gospel of work which put Carlyle or Kipling to shame. I was as faithful a wage slave as ever capitalist exploited. My joyous individualism was dominated by orthodox bourgeois ethics. . . ."

So it was with real zest that he started to shovel coal in day and night shifts, thirteen hours a day, twenty-nine days a month, for thirty dollars a month. Hour after hour, day and night, he would fill his iron wheelbarrow with coal, push it to the scales where he would weigh the load, then off to the fire room to dump the coal.

The cannery and jute mill seemed child's play compared to this; the work was so hard that even his robust frame, his "physique of twisted steel," began to break under it. He simply could not understand how human beings could be expected to work so hard. One of the firemen broke the news to him. When the superintendent saw that Jack was willing to do any amount of work to break into the trade, he had fired two men, one on the day shift and the other on the night shift, and had given the ambitious young man both of their jobs. Thus he saved fifty dollars a month.

This discovery did not cause London to quit immediately. He decided to show the superintendent that he could take it. And the loss of such a fine worker would be regretted the more deeply when he finally left. But a few days later he changed his mind. The same fireman showed him a newspaper item. It was a story of a suicide. One of the coal passers whose job Jack had unwittingly taken had killed himself, because, jobless, he could not bear watching his wife and children starve. Jack quit.

The nightmare of toil was filling in the details in Jack London's education in the class struggle. His first reaction, however, was a horror of manual labor of any sustained sort. The only choice left him by society was to kill himself by overwork or to become a tramp. He became a tramp.

This was in the spring of 1894 at a time when the ranks of the unemployed were swollen by thousands every week, when strikes of exploited workers were shaking the nation to its foundation, and when farmers were joining the chorus of national discontent in protest against forty-nine cent wheat, seven-cent cotton and twenty-six cent corn. All over the country there arose the wail of hunger from men, women and children calling upon the government to step into the situation and provide for the needs of the unemployed. But in Congress there was no awareness that the problem of unemployment and relief was any concern of the national government. "Millions for armories and the military instruction of the young," complained B. O. Flower, editor of the liberal magazine, *The Arena,* "but not one cent to furnish employment to able-bodied industry in its struggle to escape the terrible alternative of stealing or starving—such seems to be the cry of government in the United States today. . . ." Flower suggested an extensive program of public works to relieve unemployment authorized under the general welfare clause of the Constitution, a proposal which had already been advanced in December, 1893 at the convention of the American Federation of Labor.

While these ideas were being discussed in liberal magazines and at labor conventions, masses of unemployed workers were making their way by foot, rail or water to Washington, there to register emphatic dissatisfaction with the conditions of the country and to demand redress of the grievances of a whole people. From hamlet and city the armies of the Commonweal were recruited, and the spring of 1894 saw them marching down from New England, straggling in from California, Arizona and Texas, and tramping through the late snow-storms in the Alleghanies. All told about 10,000 men were on the march throughout the country with Washington as their destination.

The originator of the descent upon Washington was Jacob Sechler Coxey, a wealthy manufacturer of Massillon, Ohio who formulated a plan under which the National Government was to issue $500,000,000 in legal tender notes to be expended for the employment of citizens on a huge nation-wide road-building program. A companion measure to the good roads bill advocated issuance of legal tender notes for city streets and public buildings on the security of non-interest-bearing bonds to be authorized by any State, county or town. The two bills were introduced into Congress on March 19, 1894, by Senator Peffer, Populist, of Kansas.

Six days later Coxey's army, a "petition in boots" for the passage of the bills, left Massillon for Washington. Within a few days the idea spread like wildfire to every section of the country, and local "armies" were organized which would march across the states, picking up recruits as they went and joining Coxey in Washington. In his address to the American Railway Union Convention in June, 1894 Eugene V. Debs portrayed this mass procession in vivid language:

> *Out of work, out of money and without food, ragged, friend-less and homeless, these Commonwealers began their march to the capital city of the nation while Congress is in session. . . . Faster and still faster they rallied as the bugle call echoed through the land. They walk, they ride, they float; the storms beat upon them, their tents their skins; their couch the mother earth, their pillows stones. Some fall by the way and are buried by their comrades, unknelled and unsung, to sleep their last sleep in unknown and forgotten graves. But the survivors press forward to Washington, and as they march, recruits start up from almost every center of population in all of the land, from mountains and valley, from hill and dale, from abandoned mine and silent factory, shop and forge—they come and tramp to the muffled drum—funeral march of their throbbing hearts. The cry is, "On to Washington," where, on the marble steps of the*

> *nation's capitol, in their rags, and barefooted, they would pe-*
> *tition Congress to enact laws whereby they might perpetuate*
> *their wretched existence by toil—laws that would rekindle*
> *the last remaining sparks of hope, that their future would be*
> *relieved of some of the horrors of hunger and nakedness. . . .*

The largest of the unemployed armies was organized in San Francisco by Colonel William Baker who was soon replaced by General
Charles T. Kelly, a compositor in a San Francisco printing establishment. By April the army had recruited fifteen hundred men, "genuine
laboring men," said the San Francisco *Chronicle*, "who are now
struggling by every honest means to better their condition." On
April 7 the army sped towards Utah in freight cars. At Chautauqua
Park, Iowa, Kelly's army was joined by the eighteen-year-old Jack
London.

Jack had first made the acquaintance of Kelly's army while they
were stranded in Oakland. He mingled with the men as they marched
about the town mobilizing public support against the mayor who had
ordered them out of town and the railroad officials who had refused
to give them free transportation. He quickly decided to join the industrial army. The aims of the movement did not deeply concern
him. Here was simply a chance to see more of the world at no cost to
himself. With a ten-dollar gold piece in his pocket, contributed by his
sister Eliza, he set out for the freight yards only to find that several
hours earlier the army had been bundled into boxcars by the police,
the fire department and a contingent of deputies, and sent on its way
to Sacramento. Off he went with others who had been left behind to
catch up with the army at Sacramento, but again he missed it. Instead of turning back to Oakland, Jack decided to beat his way east
until he caught up with Kelly and his men, and then, he exulted *"On
to Washington."*

He already knew "all about this tramp business" when he started
out with his chum, Frank Davis, to pursue Kelly's army. Two years
before he had met a group of "road kids" and joined their gang to
get his first taste of the road. For several weeks he moved along with
them, beating his way across the Sierras into Nevada and back, earned
the moniker of Sailor Kid, learned to beg, to roll drunks, and the
other techniques involved in riding the freights and dodging the
bulls. He was in the company of boys who were the victims of poverty and broken homes, but his knowledge of social problems was not

greatly enhanced by this adventure. It was to be reserved for his next
hoboing experience to arouse in him an understanding of the social
and economic forces which turned men and boys into tramps. The
first indication that Jack London gives anywhere of a social consciousness is the note in his diary written a few days after he and his
companion had started out after the first detachment of Kelly's army:

> *The road has no more charms for Frank. The romance &
> adventure are gone, and nothing remains but the stern reality
> of the hardships to be endured. Though he has decided to turn
> West again I am sure the experience has done him good,
> broadened his thoughts, given him a better understanding of
> the low strata of society, & surely will have made him more
> charitable to the tramps he will meet hereafter when he is in
> better circumstances. He starts West and I start East to-
> night. . . . I Am going to brake coal on the engine from here
> to Carlin, 131 miles.*

Jack pushed eastward in box cars, in the ice box of a refrigerator
car, on the roofs of coaches, suffering from heat and cold and other
discomforts. In his penciled scrawl he noted in his diary that in the
desert "the days are burning & the nights freezing cold"; that he
"woke up at 3:30 A.M. half froze to death"; that his feet "were so
cold that it took half an hour's brisk walk to restore circulation"; that
it "was so cold on the train that night that the brakeman did not
care to bother me," and that he rode the blind baggage through a
blizzard with snow so thick that "one could not see over a rod ahead."
He also recorded the problems involved in dodging brakemen on an
Overland Limited:

> *We made a 45 mile run to Elko & a 23 mile run to Peko
> where they tried to ditch us. We went out ahead but the brake-
> man rode the blind out. We waited till the train had almost run
> by when two of us jumped the palace cars & decked them while
> the third went underneath on the rods. I climbed forward two
> cars to the other fellow & [asked him] to come on along the
> decks to the blind but he said that it was too risky. I went for-
> ward about five cars & as the brakeman was on the platform
> I could proceed no further and escape observation. I waited &
> when the train stopped I climbed down & ran ahead to the
> blind. The brakeman rode her out but I took the next one*

behind him, & when he jumped off to catch me I ran ahead &
took the platform he had vacated. The fellow on the roof with
me got ditched, but I made her into Wells, the end of the
division where they put on a double header. The brakeman was
after us like a blood hound, so I climbed on the engine &
passed coal through to Terrace, the end of that division.

When he finally caught up with Kelly and joined the rear rank of
the "first Regiment of the Reno Industrial Army," Jack found it
difficult to accept discipline and act as part of an organization. He
was still too much of an individualist to work with others for the
common good, and after all he was out for adventure, not for Congressional legislation for the unemployed. He stole out of camp each
night in violation of orders. After the army took to boats down the
Des Moines River, Jack and nine other individualists from his company went ahead of the rest. Flying American flags, they would approach a town or a group of farmers on the banks of the river, proclaim
themselves the "advance boat," dispatched by General Kelly to ar-
range for supplies, and demand provisions gathered for the army. They
took the cream of everything offered by sympathetic farmers and
townspeople, leaving the remains for the hundreds of men who arrived a half a day or a day later. For three hundred miles they lived
well, but, as Jack ruefully admitted years later, "the main army . . .
starved." Naturally, General Kelly who, unlike Jack London did not
look upon the expedition as a lark, was furious, and sent horsemen
down the banks of the river warning farmers and townspeople against
the ten pirates. Thereafter the individualists were greeted by con-
stables and dogs whenever they ran up their American flags and went
into their act. Jack and his colleagues gave up and returned to the
army.

As the going got rougher, desertions became common. And when
the army learned that on May 1st General Coxey and two other
leaders had been arrested in Washington and brought into court for
having violated "the peace and Government of the United States"
because they unlawfully entered upon the grounds of the Capitol
and "did then and there step upon certain growing plants, shrubs,
and turf . . . ," the demoralization increased. On May 18 Jack wrote
in his diary: "We passed a miserable day on the water with a chilling
wind and driving rain. In the afternoon we camped in Missouri where
we passed a miserable night." Six days later, he remarked: "We went

supperless to bed. Am going to pull out in the morning. I can't stand starvation." The next morning he deserted at Hannibal, Missouri.

Jack roamed the country as a hobo, riding the rails to Chicago, then to New York, begging for food on the way and sleeping in fields or in barns when he was not in a boxcar. His first impressions of New York were anything but pleasant. He soon became aware of the misery that lay underneath its glamor. He arrived in midsummer during a week of scorching weather. With him in the park at night were men, women and children escaping their stifling tenement rooms. The hunger and want written on their faces stayed with him for a long time.

He spent his afternoons in the City Hall Park reading damaged books which he bought from push-cart men for a few cents each and drinking ice-cold, sterilized milk sold at a penny a glass. During one of his sessions in the park a policeman approached the "meek and studious milk-drinking hobo," and, without warning, struck him a severe blow over the head with his club, knocking him down. He managed to struggle to his feet and disappear before the policeman could nab him. He had no desire to spend thirty days on Blackwells Island for resisting an officer.

A few days later Jack was in jail in Niagara Falls as a vagrant. The next morning he was sent to the Erie County penitentiary for thirty days, summarily dispatched to prison, along with fifteen other men, by a judge who did not even bother to ask a routine, "guilty or not guilty." Jack London was beginning to learn the meaning of the term, class justice. The month in prison filled in other essential details in his education in the class struggle. When he emerged from prison he knew his status in society.

Through the influence of a convict friend, Jack was made a trusty. He thus had freedom to get a complete picture of life in the Pen. He saw men robbed and beaten to death; he saw prisoners throw fits and go mad; he saw bestial tortures inflicted upon inmates by sadistic guards, and he saw the filthy, unsanitary conditions under which the prisoners were compelled to live. He saw the penal system, not reforming criminals, but actually making them worse criminals as it instilled in them the determination to revenge themselves on a society which had treated them worse than beasts. He himself ventured no protest against these conditions at this time; indeed, he acted as any other trusty, getting what he could for himself and making the convicts pay for favors. But the suffering he witnessed bit deep, and in later years he was to write brilliant, scathing indictments of prison conditions.

As soon as he was released, Jack hopped the cars of the Canadian Pacific and worked his way back to the west coast. But this was a new Jack London. The road, as he called these several months of hoboing, marks the turning point in his life. New ideas had presented themselves which were to be vastly significant in his development. The tramps he had met had treated him as an equal in spite of his youth. They had told him their stories. He had listened intently to the labor men and thinkers who were on the march with him. He learned that these men had once been as young, as strong, as fearless as he. The capitalists had used these poor "work beasts" for their gain and kicked them into the gutter or sent them to jail when they no longer provided profits. Jack saw ahead to the time when a similar fate might be his; when, instead of light-hearted vagabondage, he would be riding the rails and begging for food and shelter from necessity. He knew now that he too was a member of what the sociologists called the submerged tenth at the bottom of the social pit, and that the only way in which he could avert the scrap heap when his time came was to develop his brain, since muscles were used up so quickly.

But Jack emerged from his "life in the underworld" with more than a formula for self-elevation. The class struggle became a reality in these tramping journeys. He understood that there was something basically wrong with a society which exhausted so many people for the profits of the wealthy after which they could look forward only to misery and degradation. What if he could save himself from such a fate by playing the game properly? There would still be millions of young people like himself condemned by the existing system to the fate of the road.

As they rode the baggage cars together the men talked about these problems. Some said that there was nothing to do, for the forces which controlled society were too powerful to be beaten. But Jack heard others talk of the great strength of the working class when it was organized and how it had been able throughout history to wrest concessions from the capitalists. They spoke of socialism, of the writings of Karl Marx and Frederick Engels. In every country in the world, they told him, there existed movements based upon Marxian socialist theory which were engaged in the struggle to overthrow the present economic system and usher in a new society where the products of man's labor would be used for the benefit of all. Here in his own country, too, they assured him, there had existed such movements for nearly half a century.

American socialism before the 1890's, when Jack London became interested in the movement, had already enjoyed an exciting history. As in Europe it had its beginnings in utopian experiments founded upon the theories of Robert Owen and Charles Fourier. Marxian or Scientific Socialism was brought to the United States by German immigrants who arrived in the late 'forties and throughout the 'fifties, many of them refugees from the reaction which followed the abortive revolution of 1848. In October, 1857 the Communist Club of New York was formed with a constitution which required all members to "recognize the complete equality of all men—no matter of what color or sex," and to "strive to abolish the bourgeois property system . . . and substitute for it a sensible system under which participation in the material and spiritual pleasures of the earth would be accessible to everyone and corresponding, as much as possible, to his needs." Meanwhile, Americans were becoming familiar with the name of Karl Marx through his contributions to the *New York Tribune*, the most widely circulated newspaper in the country.

Before and during the Civil War the Marxists played a significant role in the struggle to overthrow Negro slavery and, after the war, they made their influence felt in the local and national trade unions which emerged during the course of the conflict. Yet throughout these years the growth of the socialist movement was limited by the character of its membership. It consisted mainly of German workers and intellectuals many of whom simply transferred to America what they had learned in Germany without attempting to understand the differences between the two countries. V. L. Rosenberg, Secretary of the Socialist Labor Party, put it quite candidly in 1885: "Let us not conceal the truth: the Socialist Labor Party is only a German colony, an adjunct of the German-speaking Social Democracy." A year later Engels himself criticized the German-American socialists for failing properly to integrate their movement among the American masses:

> *The Germans have not understood how to use their theory as a lever which could set the American masses in motion; they do not understand the theory themselves for the most part and treat it in a doctrinaire and dogmatic way, as some-*

thing which has got to be learnt off by heart but which will then
supply all needs without more ado. To them it is a credo, *and*
not a guide to action. Added to which they learn no English on
principle. Hence the American masses had to seek out their
own way. . . .

Despite these shortcomings, socialist thought grew enormously in
the United States during the very years Jack London was learning the
realities of the class struggle as a worker in the jute mill, cannery
and power house, and as a hobo on the road. The pent-up bitterness of
workers, farmers and small business men over the power of growing
monopoly caused them to turn an attentive ear to proposals for far-
reaching changes in the existing social system. The publication of
Edward Bellamy's *Looking Backward* in January, 1888, at the height
of the intense industrial conflict of the decade, lent impetus to this
growing interest in a new social system. Hundreds of thousands read
this utopian account of the operations of a cooperative commonwealth
in the United States in the year 2000, and overnight Nationalist
groups, seeking "to nationalize the functions of production and distribution," sprang up everywhere, linked together loosely through
correspondence and exchange of lectures, and recruiting their membership mainly from the urban middle class.

Although the short-lived Nationalist movement had little in common with scientific socialism and Bellamy himself went to great pains
to point out that he was no Marxist, it did contribute to the growth
of the socialist movement in this country. Not a few Nationalists
moved into the Socialist Labor Party (in too many cases taking with
them much more of Bellamy's utopianism and emphasis on gradual
evolutionary reforms than they did of Marxism), and *Looking Backward* continued for many years to constitute for many Americans
their first introduction to socialism.

Among those who moved from the Nationalist movement to the
Socialist Labor Party, the most important was Daniel De Leon. A
brilliant writer and a man of broad culture, De Leon rapidly became
the most prominent figure in the Socialist Labor Party. As editor of
The People, the Party's organ, and as a national lecturer for the
Party, De Leon did much to lift the Socialist Labor Party out of the
narrow confines of the German-speaking element. In the 1890's the
Socialist Labor Party still was mainly based upon foreign-born workmen, but it had set up numerous English-speaking groups. Lecturers

for the Party went all over the country to speak at "cross roads, school houses, street corners, on Commons, before debating societies, reform or radical clubs, or wherever an audience can be gathered to listen to the gospel of socialism."

The dawn of Jack London's interest in socialism coincided with the beginnings of the transformation of the socialist movement from small groups of men and women scattered about the country, who centered most of their activities around foreign-language newspapers, into a gigantic organization of protest which brought home to hundreds of thousands of the American people, through a chain of newspapers and magazines in the English language, the message that the utilization of the vast American wealth for the community rather than individual profit could produce a saner, more just and more durable society. To this remarkable growth Jack London through his writings and speeches was to make a valuable contribution.

On his return to Oakland from his tramping journey, Jack London had decided coolly and irrevocably what his course would be. Immediately he set about acquiring the formal education which, for a time, he believed indispensable to reaching his goal of selling the products of his brain. In 1895, at the age of nineteen, he entered Oakland High School. He supported himself as best he could, mowing lawns, running errands, beating carpets, and assisting the school janitor.

Still he managed to find time to pursue further the interest in socialism which the discussion on the road had aroused in him. One of his associates had often mentioned *The Communist Manifesto,* so he obtained a copy of the pamphlet from the library. He was astounded by what he read. He found all the questions that had been piling up in his mind during his life as a newsboy, factory hand, pirate and hobo clearly answered in the revolutionary pamphlet written by Marx and Engels in 1847. His own experience in the class struggle, he now saw, was no accident. He learned that throughout all history there had existed a conflict between opposing forces and that he lived in the era of the final conflict. From the pamphlet lying before him he copied into his notebook the words:

> *The whole history of mankind has been a history of contests between exploiting and exploited; a history of these class struggles shows the evolution of economic civilization just as*

> *Darwin's studies show the evolution of man; with the coming*
> *of industrialism and concentrated capital a stage has been*
> *reached whereby the exploited cannot attain its emancipation*
> *from the ruling class without once and for all emancipating*
> *society at large from all future exploitation, oppression, class*
> *distinctions and class struggles.*

He learned also, as he read further in the *Manifesto*, why previous attempts to change society into Socialism failed; how the laws of capitalist society itself force workers into organizations of their own choosing; why the bourgeoisie loses the power to remain the ruling class; and the real meaning of the so-called eternal truths like freedom and justice. He discovered, too, that there was more to the program of Scientific Socialism than a "square deal for the underdog," that it called for the abolition of private property and the collective ownership of the means of production and distribution. Now he not only began to understand the past of society, but also to see clearly the direction in which present society was moving.

One paragraph in the *Manifesto* appealed especially to Jack. He underlined with his heavy pencil the passionate words ending with the powerful battlecry:

> *The socialists disdain to conceal their aims and views. They*
> *openly declare their ends can be attained only by a forcible*
> *overthrow of all existing conditions. Let the ruling class tremble*
> *at the socialistic revolution. The proletarians have nothing to*
> *lose but their chains. They have a world to gain. Working men*
> *of all countries, unite!*

Jack never forgot these words. He used them in one form or another in street-corner speeches, in addresses before University audiences, in talks to businessmen's groups and Women's Clubs, and in his revolutionary essays, short stories and novels. He had only contempt for those socialists who wished to tone down this final paragraph of the *Manifesto*, contending that it had lost most of its original significance.

Jack London may have read little else of Marx and Engels, but it was from the *Manifesto*, with its inimitable clarity, that he obtained the fundamental concepts of his socialism. Some of the principles of Marxism that went counter to his own preconceived prejudices, he either ignored, shunted aside or distorted so that often he would mar the insight that he obtained from the *Manifesto* with absurdities. But three basic concepts which he drew from his initial reading of this pamphlet were never to leave him, even after he resigned from the Socialist Party—the belief in the class struggle; the conviction that private ownership of the means of production and the interest of the majority of the people were opposed; and confidence in the inevitable emergence of Socialism.

Now that he knew that he was a socialist, Jack began to search out the movement in his community. He joined the Henry Clay Debating Society to which came the cream of Oakland's intellectual progressives, and participated in discussions on economic issues with young lawyers, doctors, musicians and University students. He was invited to join the Socialist Labor Party branch in Oakland, became an active member, and proclaimed that his proudest possession was his Party card.

The Socialist Labor Party of Oakland had been organized in 1892 by a group of middle class intellectuals. They included a few former Abolitionists who in their quest for a new Cause had hit upon socialism, several ministers who saw in socialism a means of reviving the spirit of early Christianity, a number of exiled German socialists, and one or two former members of the British Socialist Labor Party. Much of the branch's activities was taken up with theoretical discussions, but some of the members were active propagandists, speaking on street corners and at open air meetings.

Jack participated eagerly in the discussions, but noticed the absence of workingmen. Young as he was, he had already experienced more of the class struggle than many of the members of his branch, and this, plus his reading of *The Communist Manifesto*, had convinced him that however important the middle class intellectuals were in the struggle for socialism, it would rest mainly on the shoulders of the working class to conduct the consistent class-conscious battle against capitalism. He decided to go where the workers were, attended meetings of trade unions and other workingmen's organizations, listened to the discussions and talked to them about socialism. These early contacts with the labor movement in California were to fill an important gap in his thinking. He himself had never belonged to a trade union, nor had he hitherto understood too much of the importance of organization for the working-class. Indeed, when his foster-father, John London, had worked as a scab during the great railroad strike of 1894, Jack had seen nothing to condemn in the act.

Now, however, he was to become a passionate convert to trade union-ism, and this was both to deepen his class-consciousness and to give to his writings on socialism a reality which was absent from the disser-tations of many intellectuals in the movement.

Not long after he joined the Party, Jack made his first speech in public. The Mayor of Oakland, yielding to reactionary pressure, an-nounced that there would be no more permits issued to the Socialist Labor Party for outdoor meetings. The Party decided to test the issue by conducting an outdoor meeting without a permit, leaving it up to the courts to decide the constitutionality of the Mayor's decree. Jack volunteered to speak, chancing an arrest and a possible jail sentence. But when he mounted the soap-box he got stage-fright, stammered a few incoherent sentences, and turning to his friend, Jim Whitaker, cried, "My God, Jim, I can't do it." Jim took his place. Later when a patrol wagon drew up, Jack again stepped on the soap-box, waiting to be arrested. Charged with speaking without a permit, he was let off with a stern lecture and a warning of imprisonment if it happened again.

The following day the Oakland papers played up the story, calling Jack "The Boy Socialist," a name that was picked up and applied to him for years.

All this time, Jack was at high school. He mingled little with his fellow-students, partly because they were comparatively children, and also because he was ashamed of his poor clothes and lack of money. Once he became the school janitor even the meager contacts he had established were broken.

But the existence of a student literary magazine, *The Aegis,* com-forted him. Of the ten articles and stories he published in *The Aegis,* several came from his experiences on the road and one was his first socialist article. In this essay, "Optimism, Pessimism and Patriotism," published in 1895, Jack accused the "powers that be" of keeping edu-cation from the masses, because of their fear that it would arouse in them a spirit of revolt. He pointed to the evils of capitalism, the long hours and low wages and the social and moral degradation that flowed from these evils, and urged "ye Americans, patriots and optimists to awake! Seize the reins of a corrupted government and educate the masses."

The Members of the Board of Education had barely recovered from the shock of seeing a revolutionary article in the high school paper when Jack again publicly proclaimed his socialist views before the school. Although he was not a member of the graduating class, he was chosen one of the debaters at the graduating exercises. What topic was assigned to him for his speech is not known, but immediately following his opening remarks he launched into a socialist oration. He announced his conviction that the time had arrived for the destruction of the existing social order, and that he personally was prepared to use any means to achieve this end. Georgia Bamford, one of Jack's classmates, recalls that some in the audience feared that he might at any moment descend from the platform and tear into the well-dressed listeners.

This time the Board of Education demanded disciplinary action. But Jack never returned to Oakland High School. He felt that he could learn little about writing from his English teachers who disliked his style of writing. Besides, he was twenty years old and impatient with his slow progress at school.

On money borrowed from his sister, Eliza, Jack entered a preparatory school as a short-cut to the University. He covered ground so rapidly that he was well on the way to completing two years' work in one semester. But the director, fearing that his progress would be cited by the Universities as proof of the loose methods of preparatory schools, returned Jack's fee in full. He finished the cramming by himself, studying nineteen hours a day in order to take the entrance examinations in August. For three months he dug into English, history, algebra, geometry, literature and physics, the last without the aid of a laboratory. At first he also tried to keep up with Party meetings and lectures, but after two months he gave that up to concentrate on his studies. The second week of August, 1896 saw the end of the ordeal. He spent several days at the Berkeley campus plowing through the examinations, and then, completely exhausted but confident that he had passed, took his first fling in a year and a half, getting gloriously drunk.

Jack entered the freshman class at the University of California in September and remained for little more than one semester. John London was too ill to provide for the family, and Jack had once again to shoulder the responsibilities for the home. It is doubtful, however, if he left the Berkeley campus reluctantly. He seems rapidly to have become disgusted with the superficial political and social thinking of the professors and students, and to have become convinced that there was little the faculty could teach him that he could not obtain for himself. At any rate, the bitterness he displayed later towards the cloistered life of the University campus stemmed directly from his own experience at Berkeley.

On February 4, 1897 Jack was granted honorable dismissal from the University. He knew that he had to find a job, but first he tried his hand at writing. He had contributed nothing to the publications at the University, but his name had apeared in print signed to letters he had sent to the *Times* and *Item*, Oakland newspapers, advocating socialism as against the single taxers and the Populists in the election campaign of 1896. Now he again took to the typewriter and for several weeks, working day and night, turned out poetry, essays and stories. As rapidly as he finished a manuscript he sent it off East to the magazines. But only rejection slips came back. Finally, when the London family was down to its last dollar, he gave it up and took a job in the laundry of the Belmont Academy. For thirty dollars a month plus board and lodging he sorted, washed, starched and ironed shirts, collars, cuffs and trousers. Once again he experienced the exhausting life of the wage slave; once again he was too tired after a week's work to open a book; and once again it seemed that he was trapped, doomed to have his strength sucked dry by the machine and then to be tossed aside.

Suddenly there appeared a solution to his problems. Gold was discovered in the Klondike. Adventure and the lure of easy money beckoned. On July 25, 1897, Jack and his brother-in-law, financed by Eliza to the tune of fifteen hundred dollars, most of which came from a mortgage she had taken out on her house, set sail on the *Umatilla* for the Alaskan gold fields.

Jack's Alaskan adventures would have laid the average man low forever. He wrote later of one of his feats of strength:

> *I remember at the end of the twenty-eight-mile portage across Chilkoot from Dyea Beach to Lake Linderman, I was packing up with the Indians and outpacking many an Indian. The last pack into Linderman was three miles. I back-tripped it four times a day, and on each forward trip carried one hundred and fifty pounds. This means that over the worst trails I daily traveled twenty-four miles, twelve of which were under a burden of one hundred and fifty pounds.*

He was happy in the Klondike. The men he met were congenial and stimulating, and he learned much from their discussions. To his delight he found a wide interest in the camps in political and economic issues, with socialism the favorite topic of conversation. Fred Thompson, a close companion of his Klondike days, recalled later that Jack was too busy discussing socialism with the prospectors even to split wood. These discussions around camp fires paved the way for the organization of the Socialist Party in Alaska which grew so rapidly in a few years that George Goebel, the socialist candidate, came within forty votes of being elected the first territorial representative in Congress.

Jack was deeply impressed by various aspects of life in the Klondike. He was to make frequent reference later to the fact that the Indians in Alaska shared both poverty and wealth together so that no one in the tribe benefited at the expense of others. Again he appreciated the community conscience that developed among the individualistic miners by the sheer necessities of frontier life. These men worked hard, lived hard, and fought hard, but among them there was nothing of the pettiness and sordidness of the commercial world he had left behind. Nor were they restrained by conventions. When they found gold they spent it in orgies of dissipation; yet the next night they would calmly discuss their experiences as if nothing had happened. This type of life was always to appeal to Jack London, and often, he would contrast it with civilization and its established customs. "The grim Yukon life had failed to make Daylight hard," he wrote later in his novel, *Burning Daylight*. "It required civilization to produce this result."

Yet as a socialist London understood that life in the Klondike as he knew it was doomed, and that soon enough it would give way to a new Klondike which would be more efficient than the old. He concluded an article on "The Economics of the Klondike," published in *Review of Reviews* in January, 1900, with the prediction:

> *The new Klondike, the Klondike of the future, will present remarkable contrasts with the Klondike of the past. Natural obstacles will be cleared away or surmounted, primitive methods abandoned, and the hardship of toil and travel reduced to the smallest possible minimum. Exploration and transportation will be systematized. There will be no waste energy, no harum-scarum carrying on of industry. The frontiersman will yield to the laborer, the prospector to the mining engineer, the dog-driver to the engine-driver, the trader and speculator to the steady-going modern man of business; for these are the*

men in whose hands the destiny of the Klondike will be in-
trusted.

Jack mined no gold during his year's stay in the Klondike, but he learned enough from listening to the stories of those who did the mining and from his own observations of the life about him to earn a fortune in later years. He took careful notes on everything he heard and saw and these were to provide the material for the numerous stories that were to flow from his pen after his return to the States.

An attack of scurvy hastened his homeward journey. In June, 1898, when he had recovered sufficiently to travel, Jack started on the 1900 mile voyage down the Yukon River and along the Bering Sea in a small open boat. Nineteen days later the party arrived at St. Michael where Jack got a job as a stoker on a steamer bound for British Columbia. From there he beat his way to Oakland. He arrived home penniless to find John London dead and the responsibility for the family, augmented during his absence by his foster father's grandson, completely on his shoulders.

His first impulse was to write, to turn the raw material he had gathered in Alaska into finished stories. But he shoved the desire aside and began again the search for a job. He tried everything, willing to begin as a manual laborer, willing to go back into the laundry, but all he could pick up was the usual round of odd jobs washing windows and beating carpets. When the post office announced civil service examinations, he took the tests and passed.

In the meantime, while awaiting his appointment as a mail carrier, he turned again to writing. Four years later, when his success and fame were already assured, he wrote of those early heart-breaking efforts at "Getting into Print":

> . . . . *let me state that I had many liabilities and no assets,*
> *no income, several mouths to feed, and for landlady, a poor*
> *widow woman whose imperative necessities demanded that I*
> *should pay my rent with some degree of regularity. This was*
> *my economic situation when I buckled on the harness and went*
> *up against the magazines.*
>
> *Further, and to the point, I knew positively nothing about*
> *it. I lived in California, far from the great publishing centers.*
> *I did not know what an editor looked like. I did not know a soul,*
> *with the exception of my own, who had ever tried to write*
> *anything, much less tried to publish it. . . .*

I had no one to give me tips, no one's experience to profit by. So I sat down and wrote in order to get an experience of my own. I wrote everything—short stories, articles, anecdotes, jokes, essays, sonnets, ballads, vilanelles, triolets, songs, light plays in iambic tetrameter, and heavy tragedies in blank verse. These various creations I stuck into envelopes, enclosed return postage, and dropped into the mail. Oh, I was prolific. Day by day my manuscripts mounted up, till the problem of finding stamps for them became as great as that of making life livable for my widow landlady.

All my manuscripts came back. They continued to come back. The process seemed like the working of [a] soulless machine. I dropped the manuscript into the mail box. After the lapse of a certain approximate length of time, the manuscript was brought back to me by the postman. Accompanying it was a stereotyped rejection slip. A part of the machine, some cunning arrangement of cogs and cranks at the other end . . . had transferred the manuscript to another envelope, taken the stamps from the inside and pasted them outside, and added the rejection slip.

He sent off at least seven Alaskan stories and a twenty-thousand word serial for *Youth's Companion* before he received a letter from the *Overland Monthly* to whom he had sent the story, "To the Man on the Trail." Its appearance convinced him that this was the thing he had been waiting for:

I could not open the letter right away [he wrote later]. *It seemed a sacred thing. It contained the written word of an editor. The magazine he represented I imagined ranked in the first class. I knew it had a four-thousand word story of mine. What will it be? I asked. The minimum rate, I answered modest as ever; forty dollars of course. Having thus guarded myself against any kind of disappointment, I opened the letter and read what I thought would be blazed in letters of fire on my memory for all time. Alas! the years are few, yet I have forgotten. But the gist of the letter was coldly to the effect that my story was available, that they would print it in the next number, and that they would pay me for it the sum of five dollars.*

Five dollars! A dollar and a quarter a thousand! That I did

> *not die right there and then convinces me that I am possessed of a singular ruggedness of soul which will permit me to survive and ultimately qualify me for the oldest inhabitant.*
>
> *Five dollars! When? The editor did not state. I didn't have even a stamp with which to convey my acception or rejection of his offer. Just then the landlady's little girl knocked at the back door. Both problems were clamoring more compellingly than ever for solution. It was plain there was no such thing as a minimum rate. Nothing remained but to get out and shovel coal. I had done it before and earned more money at it. I resolved to do it again. . . .*

But that very afternoon the postman brought him another letter, this time from *The Black Cat*, with the offer of forty dollars for a four-thousand-word story, provided he would consent to having it cut in half. He promptly forgot his coal-shoveling resolution, retrieved his bicycle, watch, and mackintosh from the pawnbroker, paid the landlady, the grocer and butcher, and continued "to whang away at the typewriter." The desire for self-expression, the aim to rise to the heights of literary fame completely consumed him, so that in spite of the rejection slips which followed his first success, in spite of his extreme poverty, in spite of his continued trips to the pawnbroker, when the Post Office on January 16, 1899 offered him an appointment at sixty-five dollars a month, he rejected it.

Four things, Jack decided, were necessary to become a great writer: good health, work, a philosophy of life, and sincerity. His health was good; the prodigious energy with which he attacked his writing has seldom been paralleled, but he still had to develop the clarity of his thinking and to deepen his philosophy of life. "If you think clearly," he wrote in 1903 in an article entitled "On the Writer's Philosophy of Life," "you will write clearly; if your thoughts are worthy, so will your writing be worthy. . . . If your knowledge is sparse or unsystematized, how can your words he broad or logical? And without the strong central thread of a working philosophy, how can you make order out of chaos? how can your foresight and insight be clear? how can you have a quantitative and qualitative perception of the relative importance of every scrap of knowledge you possess? And without all this how can you possibly be yourself? how can you have something fresh for the jaded care of the world?"

So he set out to systematize his thinking, to deepen his knowledge, to broaden his working philosophy of life, to "find out about this earth, this universe; this force and matter, and the spirit that glimmers up through force and matter from the maggot to Godhead," to gather up all he could of "history, evolution, ethics, and the thousand and one branches of knowledge." He read Boas and Frazer in anthropology, Darwin, Huxley and Wallace in biology, Adam Smith, Malthus, Ricardo, Bastiat, John Stuart Mill in economics, Aristotle, Gibbon, Hobbes, Locke, Hume, Hegel, Kant, Berkeley, Liebnitz, Nietzsche, Herbert Spencer, Haeckel and Kidd in history and philosophy. He reread Marx and Engels and devoured everything he could find on unemployment, the causes and cures of poverty, criminology and trade unionism.

How much of what he gulped down from these books remained with him and influenced his writing is difficult to determine exactly. But we do know that with the concepts of Marxism in his thinking were now to be amalgamated doctrines derived from Nietzsche, Spencer and Kidd.

All works on the Nietzschean world-conqueror, the strong and ruthless supermen, the blond beasts who were destined to be the rulers and emperors over all other men interested Jack London. He read and discussed several of the books by the archpriest of the cult of superman, *Thus Spake Zarathustra, The Will to Power, Genealogy of Morals, The Case of Wagner, The Antichrist,* and later wrote a preface for Leo Berg's *The Superman.* George Bernard Shaw's "philosopher-athlete" in *Man and Superman* appealed to Jack immensely.

The fact that so much of the Nietzschean philosophy, emphasizing as it did an aristocracy of supermen who would dominate the ordinary run of human beings, and flaunting its detestation of socialism and trade unionism, went counter to his socialist convictions did not bother Jack London. He took those aspects of Nietzsche which appealed to him and which he could, in his own fashion, reconcile with Marxism. After all, why could not the supermen work to bring about a system under which the average man would be benefited? "Why should there be one empty belly in all the world," he wrote in the essay "Wanted: A New Law of Development," "when the work of ten men can feed a hundred? What if my brother be not so strong as I? He has not sinned. Wherefore should he suffer hunger—he and his sinless little ones? Away with the old law. There is food and shelter for all, therefore let all receive food and shelter."

While it is true that the Nietzschean world-conqueror pops up somewhere in nearly all of his books, it still must be emphasized that London never fully accepted Nietzsche's philosophy. In his essay, "The Class Struggle," he says, speaking of the working class: "They refuse to be the 'glad perishers' so glowingly described by Nietzsche." In "How I became a Socialist," he burlesques Nietzsche's blond beast fetish: "I found there," he writes, referring to the down-and-outers among the unemployed, "all sorts of men, many of whom had once been as good as myself and just as *blond-beastly;* sailor-men, soldier-men, labor-men, all wrenched and distorted and twisted out of shape by toil and hardship and accident, and cast adrift by their masters like so many old horses." Again, in a footnote in *The Iron Heel,* London describes Nietzsche as a "mad philosopher who caught wild glimpses of truth, but who, before he was done, reasoned himself around the great circle of human thought and off into madness." Too many among London's critics have ignored these comments and have concluded that Nietzsche completely dominated his reason and conscience. Actually, London often warned against the Nietzschean philosophy, insisting that "individualism will destroy itself and will destroy America if it does not meet with Socialist opposition." Moreover, he contended that some of his most important writing was directed against Nietzsche's doctrines. Indeed, the last literary note Jack London ever penciled was to this effect: "Martin Eden and Sea Wolf, attacks on Nietzschean philosophy, which even the socialists missed the point of."

Herbert Spencer and the evolutionists of whom he was the philosophical spokesman and leader also deeply impressed Jack London. Yet, unlike the industrial and financial leaders of the country who became enthusiastic disciples of Spencer, he rejected those features of Spencer's philosophy which were used effectively against all reform movements. Whereas Spencer contended "that there shall not be a *forcible* burdening of the superior for the support of the inferior," London stressed the duty of the superior to work towards the achievement of a society which would allow all to grow to their full stature. Whereas Spencer condemned legislative interference with *natural* law, London advocated legislation outlawing factory employment of children and sweatshop wages for women workers and championed many other reforms which would eliminate evils stemming from the operation of natural law. Whereas Spencer held the rights of property to be absolute, London in speech, newspaper article, essay and book after book called for the overthrow of the system of private property.

Nothing that he read in Spencer and his disciples, Haeckel and Kidd, weakened London's belief in the inevitability of the class struggle under the capitalist system or his confidence in the ultimate triumph of socialism. From them he did obtain, however, pseudo-scientific justification for the most serious flaw in his thinking—the doctrine of white supremacy, a doctrine that was to remain with him to the end of his life. One of the persistently recurrent themes in London's stories is the supremacy over all other peoples of the white man. To the Solomon Islands on Copra and "black-birding" expeditions, to the Klondike in the grueling race for gold stakes, to the farthest north among the Eskimo tribes in Russia—over sea and mountain, sand and snow—the white man pursues through Jack London's stories his conquering way. And white man meant Nordic, and still more specifically, Anglo-Saxon. London did try to reconcile his belief in the superman with his socialism; he did reject those features of Nietzsche's and Spencer's philosophy which went counter to his conviction that all men, the strong and the weak, should unite in the struggle for socialism, but he never altered the doctrine that the white man was superior and that the earth belonged to him. There were even times when he argued that socialism was "devised for the happiness of certain kind of races," and that the socialist commonwealth should operate for the sole benefit of the Anglo-Saxon.

The amazing thing, however, is that so little of this actually entered into Jack London's writings and speeches for the socialist movement, for here he lowered the race barrier and called all men Comrades, the black and brown as well as the white. Yet perhaps it is not amazing at all, for during the most important period of his life, his activity and enthusiasm for the Cause drove out of his thinking, even if temporarily, those backward aspects of his philosophy that had no place in the make-up of a socialist. And as he drifted away from such activity and enthusiasm, they returned, weakening the validity of all that he did and wrote.

But this was still in the future. Meanwhile, he was trying desperately to make the grade as a writer. His success could be gauged by his trips to the pawnbroker. When checks from editors were scarce, Jack pawned his mackintosh and suit of clothes; when they became still scarcer, in went his bicycle, and finally when he was desperate he would turn over his typewriter. Then some story of his would be accepted, and he would redeem everything and start all over again. The following week back would go the mackintosh and suit of clothes, and in the next fortnight his bicycle and typewriter would keep them company. The *Overland Monthly* promised him seven dollars and fifty cents for every story they published, but Jack literally had to invade the office of the magazine and threaten violence before he could collect even five dollars for "The White Silence" published in February, 1899. After considerable correspondence he obtained seven-fifty each for "The Son of Wolf" which appeared in April, 1899 and "The Men of Forty Mile" the following month. With the publication of other stories, a poem and even an article or two in May and June, he was able to take his bicycle out of the pawnshop.

Twice during that terrible spring of 1899 when the family lived on beans and potatoes, when there were times that not even five cents or a slice of bread remained in the house, when he even offered to sell stories for a dollar to silence the creditors, Jack had turned down the Post Office appointment. Now it seemed that his faith in himself was justified. He was being talked about in Oakland, and even doubters had to admit that the boy with the second-hand suit and the torn mackintosh could write.

Most of the one thousand words he wrote undeviatingly every day, six days a week, went into the Alaskan stories and poems, but he also turned out socialist essays, one of which, "The Question of the Maximum," was purchased by an Eastern magazine but not published because the editor became frightened by its radical theme. Jack also used this essay as the basis of a lecture before a branch meeting of the Socialist Labor Party in Oakland. He told his comrades that the industrialized nations of the world were engaged in a race to dispose of their surplus commodities among the backward nations. Yet, since machinery was being sold to these same backward countries, they were also developing industry, even though at a slower pace, and would eventually also have a surplus. Inevitably, he predicted, great wars would occur as a result of the struggle over markets and colonies. But eventually the people would rise up and take over the means of production and distribution and put an end to the economic rivalries which led to wars. "The procession of ages," he concluded, "has marked not only the rise of man, but the rise of the common man. From the chattel slave, or the serf chained to the soil, to the highest seats in modern society, he has risen, rung by rung, amid the crumbling of the divine right of kings and the crash of falling sceptres. That he has done this, only in the end to pass into the perpetual slavery of the industrial oligarch, is something at which his whole past cries in protest. The common man is worthy of a better future, or else he is not worthy of his past."

The Oakland Socialists were so impressed with London's ability to analyze complex problems like the economic foundations of imperialism and the inevitable emergence of socialism from the contradictions within capitalism in simple, clear and vigorous language that they invited him to lecture to the Local every Sunday night. Jack promptly accepted, and although he was at his typewriter day and night trying to earn a living as a writer, he somehow managed to find the time to deliver these weekly talks. Moreover, despite his poverty he neither asked for nor expected to receive any compensation for this work.

In December, 1899 at a Socialist Labor Party meeting in San Francisco Jack first met Anna Strunsky, whose friendship during the next three years was to provide him with the intellectual stimulation that his active mind needed. She has given us an unforgettable picture of Jack London as he appeared at this time at the age of twenty-four, a picture that conveys a little of his magnetism and explains why those who once knew him could never forget him:

> I see him in pictures, steering his bicycle with one hand and with the other clasping a great bunch of yellow roses which he has just gathered out of his own garden, a cap moved back on his thick brown hair, the large blue eyes with their long lashes looking out star-like upon the world—an indescribably virile and beautiful boy, the kindness and wisdom of his expression somehow belying his youth.
>
> I see his face down among the poppies and following with his eyes his kites soaring against the high blue of the California skies, past the tops of the giant sequoias and eucalyptus which he so dearly loved.
>
> I see him becalmed on "The Spray," the moon rising behind us, and hear him rehearse his generalizations made from his studies in the watches of the night before of Spencer and Darwin. His personality invested his every movement and every

detail of his life with an alluring charm. One took his genius for granted, even in those early years when he was struggling with his unequalled energies to impress himself upon the world.

Anna was a member of a large Russian Jewish family who had come to the United States to escape the tsarist pogroms. They kept open house in San Francisco and interesting people dropped in. Jack became a frequent visitor at her home and was moved by the warmth displayed at the long dinner table. He told Anna that someday he too would like to have a large home with many guests seated about enjoying themselves. Even now his home was "the Mecca of every returned Klondiker, sailor or soldier of fortune" he had ever met. "Some day," he wrote to her, "I shall build an establishment, invite them all, and turn them loose upon each other. . . ." After learning of the coldness of his own home environment, Anna understood what motivated this desire.

With Anna Strunsky Jack was brutally frank. He was a socialist, he told her, but he was also a hard realist living in a chaotic jungle, and he was determined to push to the top. ". . . . should you know me," he wrote to her on December 21, 1899, "understand this : I, too, was a dreamer, on a farm, nay, a California ranch. But early, at only nine, the hard hand of the world was laid upon me. It has never relaxed. It has left me sentimental, but destroyed sentimentalism. It has made me practical, so that I am known as harsh, stern, uncompromising. It has taught me that reason is mightier than imagination ; that the scientific man is superior to the emotional man. . . ." His reason had convinced him, he assured her, that he could beat the capitalists at their own game, and with cold-blooded efficiency he would extract the most he could for the products of his brain. But, he insisted, this was not simply for his own personal aggrandizement, for he was confident that by so doing he would render the Cause a great service, that it would have "certain propaganda value" to show the Capitalists that "Socialists were not derelicts and failures."

Anna struggled hard to eliminate these contradictions in London's thinking, tried to get him to understand that he could not play the game of the capitalists without being corrupted by it.

This dream of his [she recalled later] *even when projected and before it became a reality, was repellent to me. The greatest natures, I thought, the surest Social Democrats, would be incapable of harboring it. To pile up wealth, or personal success—surely anybody who was a beneficiary of the Old Order must belong to it to some extent in spirit and in fact!*

So it was that our ancient quarrel, and many, many others, took their rise in the same source—a doubt, not as to himself— I never doubted the beauty and warmth and the purity of his own nature—but as to the ideas and the principles which he invited to guide his life. They were not worthy of him, I thought; they belittled him and eventually they might eat away his strength and grandeur.

She lived to see her fears justified. "He paid the ultimate price for what he received," she wrote a year after London's death. "His success was the tragedy of his life."

And success began to come. The *Atlantic Monthly* gave him the stamp of approval of the most aristocratic literary magazine in the country by purchasing his story, "An Odyssey of the North," and paying one hundred and twenty dollars for it. Then on December 21, 1899 he signed a contract with Houghton Mifflin and Company, a conservative Boston publishing house, for a volume of short stories. The reader's report on his short stories explains why his writing was overcoming the qualms and prejudices of publishers accustomed to the "prissy" literature of the day:

He uses the current slang of the mining camps a little too freely, in fact he is far from elegant, but his style has freshness, vigor, and strength. He draws a vivid picture of the terrors of cold, darkness, and starvation, the pleasures of human companionship in adverse circumstances, and the sterling qualities which the rough battle with nature brings out. The reader is convinced that the author has lived the life itself.

Then some months went by without any sales to the magazines. The pawnshop saw him again and the pinch of poverty made him cry out in despair: "It's money that I want, or rather, the things money will buy: and I can never possibly have too much." Still he turned out articles on socialism that he knew no magazine would touch and continued studying for future essays on the same subject. At the same time he made speaking tours for the Party to Alameda, San Jose, and other towns. His work for the magazines was hack-work but the time he devoted to the Party was spent on work that he loved, and he was completely frank with himself. On February 3, 1900 he wrote to Anna Strunsky: "Saturday night, and I feel good. Saturday night, and a good week's work done—hack work, of course. Why shouldn't I. Like any other honest artisan by the sweat of my brow. . . ."

He felt good, too, for still another reason. For some time Jack had been longing for a home, children, and respectability. Frustrated in his desire to marry his first love, Mabel Applegarth, he proposed to Bessie Maddern whom he had known for some time and who, he objectively concluded, would make a good wife and an intelligent companion. Bessie like Jack loved someone else, but like him, too, she was lonely and anxious for her own home. She accepted his proposal and a week later, in January, 1900, they were married.

The turn of the century found Jack's luck definitely changed for the better. *McClure's Magazine* bought two of his short stories and agreed to take all he could turn out. In April his first volume of short stories, *The Son of the Wolf,* was published. The critics hailed him as "a natural born story teller," said the book was "full of fire and feeling," and that it possessed "much of the imaginative power and dramatic force of Kipling," with a "tenderness of sentiment and quick appreciation of the finer sentiments of heroism that are seldom seen in Kipling." The book sold fairly well and McClure promptly agreed to advance Jack $125 a month while he worked on a full-length novel.

Marriage, his wife's pregnancy and the widening circle of friends who dropped in on him at all times put a heavy drain on his allowance from McClure and the royalties from his first book. So, in addition to his daily stint on the novel, he was forced to turn out light verse, humorous sketches, stories and reviews. He also found time to win the first prize of two hundred dollars in a contest sponsored by *Cosmopolitan Magazine* for the best article on "Loss by Lack of Co-operation" with a socialist essay, "What Communities Lose by the Competitive System." Jack had toned down the article to fit the mood of the editors and it hardly breathes the revolutionary fervor to be found in his later essays. Still it is a logical and calm appraisal of the evils of the competitive system, showing how competition makes for duplication of work, and why, because of the waste growing out of this duplication, a planned society is necessary. The essay was reprinted as a penny pamphlet by the Socialist Party of England.

On January 15, 1901 his daughter, Joan, was born. It took Jack some time to recover from his disappointment at not having a son,

but the need to finish the novel drove everything else out of his mind.
A few weeks after Joan was born the manuscript was forwarded to
McClure. Both author and publisher agreed that it was a disappoint-
ing work. McClure decided not to publish the book, but to retrieve
some of his investment, peddled it around among other houses and
finally sold it to J. B. Lippincott and Company of Philadelphia under
whose imprint it appeared in October, 1902.

The Daughter of the Snows, London's first novel, did not enhance
his reputation, yet it is important in revealing certain trends in his
writing. Frona Welse, the heroine of the book, returns to her home
in Alaska after several years at school. The reader first meets her
as she is being rowed from the steamer to the Alaskan town she has
not seen in years, and immediately he is brought into contact with a
new type of American heroine. Any other of the 1902 type would
have blushed and fainted at the oaths and blasphemies poured out by
the boatmen, but Frona is at home with them. Actually, she can hold
her own with them in the toughest of work.

Through the character of her father, Jacob Welse, the trader, the
reader grasps London's love of the community spirit on the frontier.
When a famine threatens the miners, Welse says: "A Bonanza property, or a block of Bonanza properties, does not entitle you to a
pound more than the oldest penniless 'sour-dough,' or the newest baby
born. Trust me. As long as I have a pound of grub you will not starve.
Stiffen up. Shake hands." Here is the frontier emphasis on a man's
need rather than his possessions which London regarded so superior
to what he saw in more civilized society.

From this high level of social thinking London descends to his
doctrine of white supremacy. During a discussion Frona Welse ex-
presses her belief in the superiority of the white man over the natives,
pointing out that the white man had always been able to best the
Indian. London not only permits her to win the argument but later has
Vance Corliss, who originally disagreed with Frona, echo her views.
In essence, they are the views of London himself.

The publication of *The Daughter of the Snows* marks the end of
the first and most minor period in London's career as a writer. Before
its appearance two other volumes of his short stories, *The God of His
Fathers* and *Children of the Frost*, had come off the press. Three
volumes of short stories and one novel in three years was no mean
achievement for a young writer. Jack London was definitely on his
way, but his greatest work still lay before him.

During these years when Jack London was striving to become a successful writer the socialist movement in the United States was undergoing important changes. It had gained a remarkable new leader when Eugene V. Debs embraced socialism and it operated through a new organization when the Socialist Party of the United States was formed.

Until the Pullman strike of 1894 Debs had been convinced that through progressive trade unionism the working class would be able to abolish poverty, unemployment, injustice and all of its other grievances. But the ruthlessness of the railroad companies and the eager cooperation of the national government in breaking the strike opened his eyes. As Debs himself put it: ". . . in the gleam of every bayonet and the flash of every rifle *the class struggle was revealed.*" Later, while in jail for having defied an injunction during the strike, he read many books and pamphlets dealing with social and economic problems, including the first volume of Marx's *Capital.* He emerged from jail a confirmed socialist.

In the election of 1896 Debs campaigned for William Jennings Bryan, believing "that the triumph of Mr. Bryan and free silver would blunt the fangs of the money power." Following McKinley's election, he devoted all of his time and energy to the socialist movement. When the Brotherhood of the Co-operative Commonwealth—a utopian scheme for colonizing some western states—was formed in the fall of 1896, Debs became the chief organizer. In June, 1897 he united the remnants of the American Railway Union and the Brotherhood of the Co-operative Commonwealth to form the Social Democracy of America. In a circular letter to his associates in the labor movement, he wrote:

> *The issue is Socialism versus Capitalism. I am for socialism because I am for humanity. We have been cursed with the reign of gold long enough. Money constitutes no proper basis of civilization. The time has come to regenerate society—we are on the eve of a universal change.*

Two months after the founding of the new party, the Jewish socialists of the East joined its ranks. These socialists had long been chafing under the domination of Daniel De Leon and the philosophy of the Socialist Labor Party under his leadership. They were opposed to De Leon's dual union tactics, his indifference to immediate demands,

44   JACK LONDON

his subordination of the Party to the industrial organization of the workers and his intransigence and inability to work with anyone who did not unreservedly accept his doctrines. Furthermore, the lawyers and middle class intellectuals among the Jewish socialists shared none of De Leon's revolutionary zeal and writhed under his attacks against petty bourgeois elements in the Party. In the 1896 convention of the Socialist Labor Party the Jewish socialists had been expelled because of their opposition to some of De Leon's policies. In August, 1897 they voted to affiliate with the Social Democracy of America.

In the summer of 1898 a split occurred in the Social Democracy over the colonization plan. The anti-colonizationists favoring political action were defeated at the party's convention, but they bolted and decided to organize a new socialist party to be composed only of those who believed in the "principles and program of International Socialism." The group adopted as its name, The Social Democratic Party of America. Debs went along with the bolters and toured the country for the new party.

For a while there was hope that the Social Democratic Party and the Socialist Labor Party would amalgamate and form a united socialist movement. Indeed, in order to promote the fusion, the National Executive Board of the Social Democratic Party, of which Debs was a member, requested the editor of its official organ not to accept articles which attacked either the tactics or the personnel of De Leon's organization. But the unity movement quickly dissolved. A major break was occurring in the Socialist Labor Party as members everywhere rose up in revolt against the dictatorial methods of De Leon and his sectarian policies. Early in 1900 these discontented elements, led by Morris Hilquit, Job Harriman and Max Hayes, met in Rochester, New York, appointed a committee to work for unification with the Social Democratic Party and invited that organization to appoint a committee for the same purpose. The Social Democratic Party first referred to its membership the question: "Is union between the Social Democratic Party and the Socialist Labor Party faction desirable?" The vote, announced in May, 1900, was 939 for union and 1213 against. Nevertheless, the forces working for unity persisted and temporary fusion was achieved with two separate Social Democratic Parties functioning. In the political campaign of 1900 Debs was nominated for President of the United States by both groups and polled nearly a hundred thousand votes.

A year later those who had worked for a united socialist movement saw their hopes realized. In August, 1901, a resolution was adopted at a convention in New York attended by delegates from both groups proclaiming the birth of the new Socialist Party under the leadership of Eugene V. Debs, Victor Berger, and Morris Hilquit.

All of these developments since 1896 barely touched the socialist movement in Oakland and San Francisco. As far as Jack London himself was concerned we have only one statement which indicates any reaction on his part to what was taking place in the movement nationally. When the Social Democracy of America was first formed by Eugene V. Debs in June, 1897, he wrote to Ted Applegarth: "Organized labor headed by Debs and beginning with the American Railway Union, has commenced a change of front. The old methods of strikes and boycotts to obtain shorter hours and better pay has been abandoned. They now strike for political power, their openly avowed goal being the cooperative commonwealth. That is, the socialist propaganda in the United States is assuming greater proportions." It is hardly an acute observation and, as was to happen frequently in the future, Jack was allowing his imagination to run away with his judgment, but it does reveal that his interest in the movement was growing. Thereafter he expressed no views on the issues involved in the conflict inside the Socialist Labor Party, but he must have been a follower of Debs, for whom he had the greatest respect and admiration, and when the great majority of the Oakland Socialists left the Socialist Labor Party and affiliated with the Socialist Party, Jack London went along with them.

In 1901 the newly-organized Oakland Socialist Party nominated Jack London, already its most popular and most publicized member, for mayor. In accepting the nomination, the twenty-five-year-old candidate said: "It is we, the Socialists, working as a leaven throughout society, who are responsible for the great and growing belief in municipal ownership. It is we, the Socialists, by our propaganda, who have forced the old parties to throw as sops to the popular unrest certain privileges." Jack put up a good campaign, but he only gained a meager 245 votes.

If the voters of Oakland had read a story by Jack London published about the time he was running for mayor the chances are that he would have received still fewer votes. Irving Stone characterizes "The Minions of Midas" which appeared in *Pearson's Magazine* in

May, 1901, as a "proletarian" story and hails it as initiating socialist fiction writing in America. Actually, although the story contains phrases like "wage slaves," "Capitalist Class," and "industrial and social wrong," it is anything but "proletarian" in content and orientation and is more revealing of some of London's limitations as a socialist than of his contribution to socialist fiction.

The story is composed of seven letters written to the Money Baron, Eben Hale, by anonymous members of a class-conscious organization calling itself The Minions of Midas. They ask for twenty million dollars and promise to strike down various innocent people if he spurns their demand. In the midst of these murders, Eben Hale, who has refused to be intimidated, commits suicide.

The members of this terroristic organization may have been class-conscious wage-slaves, but their goal is purely a selfish one. They believe that because of their superiority they should be co-rulers of the earth along with the capitalists. They are not interested in changing society; they merely want to share the spoils with the capitalists and, to achieve this goal, they institute a reign of terror to mulct the millionaires of a large portion of their wealth. Nowhere is there even the slightest indication that this money will be used to right social evils. The group simply wants the money because it needs capital to compete with the great trusts and business combinations of the capitalists.

The Minions of Midas refer to themselves as "a new force" in society, but they have nothing in common with the real force emerging at this time represented by the labor and socialist movements. Indeed, those who were slandering trade unionists and socialists, charging that they sought to achieve their aims by the murder of innocent people, could have made good use of Jack London's so-called "proletarian" story.

Probably London tossed the story off as a piece of hack-writing or perhaps he gained a certain satisfaction from the idea that The Minions of Midas were fulfilling his own personal ambition of beating the capitalists at their own game. At any rate, the story reveals how much he had yet to learn as a socialist. There were one or two members of the Socialist Party of Oakland who recognized these weaknesses in London's thinking even at this early stage in his career and tried to influence him to eradicate them. But their voices were drowned in the chorus of approval that arose from the hero-worshipping elements in the Party, most of whom knew little of Marxism themselves, and were impressed by the thought that London was reaching circles with the socialist message that they could never approach.

This much, at least, is true. Jack London was being invited to talk to groups never before reached by the socialists on the Pacific Coast. He may have made few converts on such occasions, but he did reveal his contempt for the bourgeoisie in no uncertain terms. He was invited to speak to the Women's Press Association of San Francisco on Rudyard Kipling, and a crowded auditorium faced the handsome young writer when he arose to speak. He calmly told the distinguished audience that he had sent his article on Kipling to a magazine and, since he could not speak without his manuscript, he would talk to them on "The Tramp."

This lecture had originally been delivered before the Alameda Socialist Party, was to be published in *Wilshire's Magazine,* an independent socialist monthly in February-March, 1904, and was to appear in book form a year later as the second essay in *The War of the Classes.*

To the Women's Press Association, London demonstrated, by marshalling an array of facts, that the tramp was in reality a product of economic necessity, fulfilling a need in capitalist society. The army of surplus labor, he told the ladies, is needed when production increases and the ordinary workers cannot handle the work ; it is needed to work on emergency projects and to meet the demands of seasonal employment, and finally, but most important, it is needed to act as a check on all employed labor. "That which maintains the integrity of the present industrial society," he declared, "more potently than the courts, police, and military is the surplus labor army." For if it did not exist, there would be no limit to what the workers might demand, and before long labor would control both the means of production and the state. The surplus army, he continued, is recruited from the less efficient workers who can no longer provide a profit for their employers, and from those who are thrown out of work because of an economic crisis or technological improvements. They had the choice of becoming actual slaves, by working for whatever pittance their employers will toss them, or going on the road. Many of them choose to become tramps, rebels against the social order that compelled them to follow this course.

London concluded his talk with a brilliant piece of satire. He saw but one way out of the dilemma confronting society arising from the existence of the surplus army—kill off this army and then there will be no unemployment and no tramps. But the ethics of capitalism forbids this; yet it is perfectly ethical to leave them to starve to death. So let them live. But don't tell the tramp to go to work: "As the scapegoat to our economic and industrial sinning, or to the plan of things, if you will, we should give him credit. Let us be just. He is so made. Society made him. He did not make himself."

When the lecture was published several socialists pointed to significant omissions in the brilliant analysis of unemployment in capitalist society and indicated that, instead of emphasizing the struggles of the oppressed classes, London stressed their helplessness in the hands of society. But the staid ladies of the Women's Press Association were too horrified to worry about such details. When the lecture ended, the audience was in an uproar. The well-dressed listeners attacked London with such heat that the Chairlady hurriedly adjourned the meeting to prevent fist-fights.

On July 21, 1902 London received a wire from the American Press Association asking if he were ready to go immediately to South Africa to report on the aftermath of the Boer War which had come to a close six weeks before. Jack leaped at the chance, accepted by telegraph within an hour, and left immediately for New York. On arriving in the Empire City he headed for the offices of the Macmillan Company, met George F. Brett, its president, and told him about the Kempton-Wace letters, a series of philosophical letters on love on which he and Anna Strunsky had been working for some time, and which is interesting today solely because they provide an excellent insight into London's backward ideas on women. Brett promptly accepted it for publication, and assured Jack that when he returned from South Africa Macmillan would publish all that he wrote.

In high spirits, Jack sailed on the *Majestic* for England. His jubilant frame of mind was due to more than his arrangement with Macmillan and the prospect of adventure that lay before him. His trip east had convinced him that the Cause was making progress. "I meet the men of the world in Pullman coaches, New York clubs, and Atlantic liner smoking rooms," he wrote to Anna Strunsky his second day on the boat, "and, truth, to say, I am made more hopeful for the Cause by their total ignorance and non-understanding of the forces at work. They are blissfully ignorant of the coming upheaval, while they have grown bitterer and bitterer towards the workers. You see, the growing power of the workers is hurting them and making them bitter while it does not open their eyes." In the same letter, Jack outlined his plan of operation during his stay in London. For two days he would sink out of sight in the slums of the East End, to view the coronation of King Edward from the standpoint of the slum people.

The two days were to stretch into six weeks. When the ship docked, Jack was handed a cablegram from the Press Association cancelling the engagement. He was left with a return ticket, but with little money. Still Jack decided that it was a fortunate turn of events, for now he could really examine the slums of London about which he had heard and read so much.

Passing as an American sailor stranded in England, Jack bought some second-hand clothes, rented a room in the East End and then set out to investigate life in the slums, taking with him the criteria— "That which made for more life, for physical and spiritual health, was good; that which made for less life, which hurt, dwarfed, and distorted life, was bad." Out of that experience came the terrible picture of poverty and misery, *The People of the Abyss*. It was a book which was turned out white-hot from the boiling reservoirs of Jack London's indignation. Speaking of it in a letter to a friend, he says, "It is rather hysterical, I think," but in later years he is said to have loved it most of all his books, because "no other book of mine took so much of my young heart and tears as that study of the economic degradation of the poor."

Though the book is replete with factual data which lend authenticity to the study, London was not content merely to survey the scene as a sociologist, calmly taking notes and then presenting an academic analysis of conditions. He got to know the people; he talked with them, and knocked about with the sailor, the hop-picker, the derelict and the pauper. ". . . I was out all night with the homeless ones," he wrote to Anna Strunsky on August 25, 1902, "walking the streets in the bitter rain, and, drenched to the skin, wondering when dawn would come. Sunday I spent with the homeless ones, in the fierce struggle for something to eat. I returned to my rooms Sunday evening, after thirty-six hours continuous work and short one night's sleep. . . . I am worn out and exhausted and my nerves are blunted with what I have seen and the suffering it has cost me." His friend Upton Sinclair reported that "for years afterwards the memories of this stunted and depraved population haunted him beyond all peace."

London visited rooms which were mean, sordid and completely lacking in sanitation, and learned that the people who occupied these dwellings earned so little in return for back-breaking and heart-breaking toil that they could barely keep body and soul together; that the mortality rate in "this human hell-hole" was appalling. Suicides were so common that they passed unnoticed. Many of the slum dwellers lived for drink alone, but London points out that it was the misery of their lives that drove them to drink, crime and suicide.

But there were those who were worse off than the slum dwellers, the completely destitute who were without even the security of a filthy room. They were condemned to "Carrying the Banner," that is, walking the streets by night, routed out of every corner by the policeman's club. Some slept in the parks or on the benches along the Thames Embankment. Others waited in line long, dreary hours at workhouses for a chance at a mean cot, often to hear the callous cry, "Full-up," as they were about to approach the door. Then they departed for another workhouse where, too often, they met with the same response. London tells of one occasion, when after being turned away from one workhouse, he set out with a carter and a carpenter for another. The men had once been skilled workers, earning a fair living, but they were now too old to produce a profit for any employer. As they walked along, London noticed:

> *From the slimy, spittle-drenched side-walk, they were picking up bits of orange peel, apple skin, and grape stems, and they were eating them. The pits of green gage plums they cracked between their teeth for the kernels inside. They picked up stray crumbs of bread the size of peas, apple cores so black and dirty one would not take them to be apple cores, and these things these two men took into their mouths, and chewed them, and swallowed them; and this, between six and seven o'clock in the evening of August 20, year of our Lord 1902, in the heart of the greatest, wealthiest, and most powerful empire the world has ever seen.*

London was extremely critical of the workhouses. For a cot and a bit of supper and breakfast consisting of food unfit for human consumption, they worked the wretched men nearly to death. The Salvation Army operated a superior type of workhouse, but before one could get any food, he had to wait in line for two hours and another hour inside. Then he was forced to pray and listen to pious speeches before a scanty breakfast was served. Small wonder so many of these destitute men and women would go without food for days on end. Many became ill as their resistance to the rampant slum diseases was lowered. Once ill, their chances for recovery were negligible.

Throughout his investigation London sought an answer to the question, why are these people in the slums? Not by choice and not through laziness, he discovered, but old age, disease, or accidents which had reduced their labor value. Escape from the slums was difficult, for the tiny wages of these people simply did not permit them to live elsewhere. Then when they were thrown on society's scrap heap, through illness, age, accident, they had no resources on which to draw. Slow starvation was the common end.

This picture of the slums was obtained, moreover, in what was considered "good times," when business was prosperous, when the factory hands and the clerks were "normally" employed. "The starvation and lack of shelter I encountered," London wrote, "constituted a chronic condition of misery which is never wiped out, even in the periods of greatest prosperity."

London was not content simply to paint a devastating picture of the life of the poor. As a socialist he drew conclusions which the ordinary social worker or academician was wont to ignore. He compared the inhabitants of the British Isles with the primitive Indians of Alaska. Among the Innuit folks who lived along the banks of the Yukon River, he pointed out, chronic starvation is unknown. When there was a lack of food, all suffered; when there was plenty, all ate their fill. But in the civilized world one had too much and another too little. One man lived in a fine mansion, another slept in some dark doorway. Everywhere there was starvation in the midst of plenty.

> *The unfit and the unneeded!* [he wrote bitterly]. *The miserable and despised and forgotten, dying in the social shambles. The progeny of prostitution—of the prostitution of men and women and children, of flesh and blood, and sparkle and spirit; in brief, the prostitution of labor. If this is the best that civilization can do for the human, then give us howling and naked savagery. Far better to be a people of the wilderness and desert, of the cave and the squatting place, than to be a people of the machine and the Abyss.*

Why is it, London asked, that as civilization increased its producing power misery increased in direct ratio? The cause was mismanagement; the answer a socialist commonwealth. The profit motive must go. Society must be compelled to better the lot of the average man, capable as it is of a production of abundance. Society must be re-organized on a basis of production for use and not for profit. Once capitalist mismanagement is wiped out, the evil of the slums, of slow starvation, of disease, of death from malnutrition, will be wiped off the face of the earth.

The People of the Abyss, published by Macmillan in November, 1903, received mixed reactions from the critics. *The Nation* commented that London "describes the East End of London as Dante might have described the Inferno had he been a yellow journalist." The *Atlantic Monthly* considered it "deficient in the firmness and dignity of mood and touch which might have made it literature," while the *Bookman* accused the author of "snobbishness because of his profound consciousness of the gulf fixed between the poor denizens of the Abyss and the favored class of which he is the proud representative. . . ."

Other critics recognized the book for what it was, a major sociological study of the underprivileged deserving to stand besides Jacob Riis' *How the Other Half Lives* and Arthur Morrison's *Tales of Mean Street.* "This life," said *The Independent,* "has been pictured many times before—complacently and soothingly by Professor Walter A. Wyckoff, luridly by Mr. Stead, scientifically by Mr. Charles Booth. But Mr. London alone has made it real and present to us." A few months after the American publication of the book, Isaac Pitman's Sons, a conservative London publishing house, brought out a British edition. The English critics were favorably impressed, and agreed that Jack London had come closer to the heart of the East End slums than any other writer.

The People of the Abyss brought Jack London to the attention of the entire socialist movement in the United States. Previous to its appearance he was only well-known on the Coast. Then *Wilshire's* printed *The People of the Abyss* serially, beginning with the March, 1903 issue and running it through January, 1904. Thus several months before Macmillan released the book, socialists all over the country were reading London's burning indictment against capitalism, and overnight his name became a household word among Party members.

Jack London returned to California four months after he had left for England to pick up the responsibilities of a family man. In the winter of 1902 he was again the father of a daughter, and his disappointment at not having been presented with a son by Bessie made both of them ill. Then an idea for a story possessed him, and he forgot mother and daughter, and once again was at work nineteen hours a day, his only recreation being the Wednesday night open house for his friends.

In June, 1902, *Cosmopolitan* had published "Batard," London's story of a struggle between a dog, uncanny in his diabolic shrewdness, and his evil master, each biding his time to kill the other, each fearing and respecting the other to the end. Now he sat down to write a short story that would be a companion piece to "Batard." But what started out to be a four thousand word story grew into a full-length novel, which London, who had a genius for selecting just the right title, named *The Call of the Wild*. It was completed in thirty days and accepted immediately by the *Saturday Evening Post* which paid him two thousand dollars for the month's work. Though Brett of Macmillan liked the story, he did not care for the title and feared that the novel was too realistic to be popular with "the sentimentalist public." He, therefore, proposed that London sell the book outright to Macmillan for two thousand dollars, with the assurance that it would be published in an attractive format and heavily advertised. This, in turn, would increase the sale of London's books already published. The need for money to support his family, two servants and Mammy Jenny brought from Jack a quick acceptance of the offer.

It is not difficult to understand Brett's doubts about the success of *The Call of the Wild*. (It remained the title for the simple reason that no better one was proposed.) A generation brought up on animal stories like *Black Beauty* and familiar with the quaint animal characters of the *Uncle Remus Stories* of Joel Chandler Harris, was likely to be shocked at the savagery of the story of Buck, a cross between a St. Bernard and a Scotch-shepherd, who led the life of an ordinary dog until he was kidnapped and taken to the Klondike, and who, when the call of the wild asserted itself after the death of his master, is drawn back to life with the wolf-pack. But the publisher had overlooked the fact that the increased interest in natural history stimulated by men like Muir and Burroughs, and the growing taste for realism in literature, had created an audience for just such a type of story. Then again, the novel is endowed with such magic and imagination, it moves so swiftly to its logical end, and recreates so brilliantly the atmosphere appropriate to the moods of the animals, that no reader could possibly be unmoved. Thousands were soon to thrill to the struggle between Buck and Spitz for leadership of the team, to the picture of the Arctic code of survival, to the huskies' "pride of the trace," and to the bitter rivalry which culminated in a battle to the death. Finally, there were passages of beauty, the equal of which it is difficult to find in the literature of the day such as:

> *With the aurora borealis flaming coldly overhead, or the stars leaping in the frost dance, and the land numb and frozen under its pall of snow, the song of the huskies might have been the defiance of life, only it was pitched in a minor key, with long-drawn wailings and half sobs, and was more the pleading of life, the articulate travail of existence. It was an old song, old as the breed itself—one of the first songs of the younger world in a day when songs were sad. It was invested with the woe of unnumbered generations, this plaint by which Buck was so strangely stirred. When he moaned and sobbed, it was with the pain of living that was of old the pain of his wild fathers, and the fear and mystery of the cold and dark that was to them fear and mystery.*

Fortunately, the usual interpolations about white supremacy which mar so much of London's work are absent in this book. In fact, it is interesting in the light of his phobia about mixed breeds that London's brave and dignified dog hero should be a mongrel!

The critical response to *The Call of the Wild* was so overwhelmingly favorable that ten thousand copies were sold the first day of publication. It was the first of London's books to be a best seller, and it remains today the best known of his writings, having sold over six million copies since 1903.

A month before *The Call of the Wild* was published, *The Critic* carried an article by London, "The Terrible and Tragic in Fiction." It concluded with a remark that was to loom large in London's future development. "The pity of it," he wrote, "is that the writer-folk are writing for bread first and glory after; and that their standard of living goes up as fast as their capacity for winning bread increases,— so that they never get around to glory,—the ephemeral flourishes, and the great stories remain unwritten." *The Call of the Wild* assured London the status of a highly paid author, yet the more money he made the more he was to need with the result that in the end he turned out material that had value only because it made money, and the great stories in him also remained unwritten.

But that was to come much later. Meanwhile, he still devoted no small part of his writing time to work for the radical movement, for which he received nothing but the satisfaction of knowing that he was aiding the Cause.

The Comrade, an official Party publication founded in 1901 * was featuring a series of articles by well-known Party members on how they became Socialists. There were contributions by Father McGrady, the Rev. T. H. Hagerty, William T. Brown, Joshua Wanhope and other prominent socialists of the period. Naturally, Jack London was asked for his story, and in "How I Became a Socialist" he told of his experiences on the road, of his gradual realization of the fact that society took men of brawn and muscle, used them up and discarded them, and of his fear that someday this too would be his fate. He told how his rebellion against this system made him investigate possible cures, and led him to socialism. Since that day, he told his Party comrades, he had read many books on the subject, "but no economic argument, no lucid demonstration of the logic and inevitableness of Socialism affects me as profoundly and convincingly as I was affected on the day when I first saw the walls of the Social Pit rise around me and felt myself slipping down, down, into the shambles at the bottom."

The essay brought a flood of demands for articles from the socialist press and large batches of mail from comrades all over the country. Jack responded to both. For the socialist press he wrote a series of articles without either expecting or receiving any financial return. He personally answered every letter from comrades, opening each with "Dear Comrade," and closing, "Yours for the Revolution, Jack London." Two of the socialist essays written during this period illustrate Jack London's ability to take a difficult subject and so simplify it that even a political illiterate could understand it. Furthermore, they reveal his capacity for applying Marxism to American conditions.

In "The Class Struggle," published in the New York *Independent* of November 5, 1903, London sets out to destroy one of the cherished myths of American capitalism: that there is no class struggle in

---

* After reading the first issue of the magazine, London wrote joyfully to the editor: "My congratulations on your noteworthy first number. What with the *International Socialist Review* and *The Comrade,* I really feel a respectable member of society, able to say to the most finicky: 'Behold the literature of my party!' But, seriously, I must confess to a pleasant surprise at the work you have done." (*The Comrade,* November, 1901, Vol. I, no. 2, p. 32.)

American society. The believers in the myth are like ostriches with
their heads in the sand; because they cannot see the class struggle,
they refuse to recognize that it exists. He points out that the disap-
pearance of the frontier forced the superior workers, who usually rose
out of their class, to remain in the working class. At first they seek to
improve their conditions through individual efforts, but life teaches
them that as individuals they are powerless to combat the system
which exploits them. So they begin to play a leading role in the organization of labor, and soon these "ambitious young men, denied
the opportunity to rise from the working class, preach revolt to the
working class." The existence of trade unions, London argues, is
irrefutable proof of the presence of the class struggle. Capital wants
more profit and labor wants higher wages, and no amount of pretty
speechifying about the need for harmony between these two classes
can blunt the basic struggle that exists between them. In this struggle,
London is convinced, the workers will win out as soon as they understand that their class has little or nothing to gain from the old-line
political parties, build their own and take over control of the government. London is aware that many of the existing trade unions do not
understand that trade unionism divorced from political activity is
often futile, and he does not hesitate to call this to the attention of
the American labor movement. Trade unionism coupled with a correct political ideology, he concludes, will achieve a new social order
in America.

"The Scab," published in the *Atlantic Monthly* in January, 1904, is
further evidence of London's concern with major problems confronting the working class. Here again he stresses the existence of a class
struggle between labor and capital, and shows how the scab is an
inevitable feature of this struggle. Unfortunately, as the essay develops, its power dwindles. London's definition of a scab takes in so
much territory that one cannot be sure just what he has in mind. A
scab, he argues, "is one who gives more value for the same price than
another." He differentiates, to be sure, between the scab who is
utilized by employers to break strikes and a laborer who does more
work for the same wage than another. But the difference is somewhat
glossed over in the discussion, and the reader is led to the conclusion
that almost everybody scabs in a society where men struggle with one
another for food and shelter—worker against worker, capitalist
against capitalist and nation against nation. In fact, London concludes
that in a competitive society "the non-scab is a vanishing quantity."

In addition to the loose terminology, London's essay also suffers
from a failure to analyze sufficiently the reasons why men scab on their
fellow-workers. While he points out that the employers use scabs
to destroy the organized power of labor, he leaves the impression that
their main aim is to get low-paid workers, thus overlooking the fact
that professional strike-breakers were being paid more for a month's
work than the men on strike received during the entire year. Nor does
he point out that the refusal of the craft unions to organize Negro
and women workers often lead them to scab against their will.

Despite these weaknesses, however, the essay remains an important
theoretical discussion of a phenomenon extremely common "in a
society organized on a tooth-and-nail basis." At a time when Charles
Elliot, President of Harvard University, was calling the scab "the
American hero," Jack London was demonstrating that the strikebreaker was simply another mercenary in the army of the capitalists
to crush the organizations of labor.

Some time later London wrote a description of a scab which, though
it never could have found a place in the pages of the *Atlantic Monthly,*
provided the labor movement with an eloquent and forceful weapon
in its struggles and is still widely used today:

> *After God had finished the rattlesnake, the toad and the vam-*
> *pire, he had some awful substance left with which He made a*
> *SCAB. A SCAB is a two-legged animal with a corkscrew soul,*
> *a water-logged brain, and a combination backbone made of*
> *jelly and glue. Where others have hearts he carries a tumor of*
> *rotten principles.*
>
> *When a SCAB comes down the street men turn their backs*
> *and angels weep in heaven, and the devil shuts the gates of hell*
> *to keep him out. No man has a right to SCAB as long as there*
> *is a pool of water deep enough to drown his body in, or a rope*
> *long enough to hang his carcass with. Judas Iscariot was a*
> *gentleman compared with a SCAB. For betraying his Master,*
> *he had character enough to hang himself. A SCAB HASN'T!*
>
> *Esau sold his birthright for a mess of pottage. Judas Iscariot*
> *sold his Savior for thirty pieces of silver. Benedict Arnold*
> *sold his country for a promise of a commission, in the British*
> *Army. The modern strikebreaker sells his birthright, his coun-*
> *try, his wife, his children, and his fellow-men for an unfulfilled*
> *promise from his employer, trust or corporation.*

Esau was a traitor to himself, Judas Iscariot was a traitor to his God. Benedict Arnold was a traitor to his country.

A STRIKEBREAKER IS A TRAITOR TO HIS GOD, HIS COUNTRY, HIS FAMILY AND HIS CLASS!

In the summer of 1903, London fell in love with Charmian Kittredge and abruptly left his wife and two daughters. Then he settled down to the writing of *The Sea Wolf*. On January 7, 1904, five days before his twenty-eighth birthday, he sailed for Yokohama on the *S.S. Siberia* to cover the Russo-Japanese war for the Hearst syndicate, leaving the manuscript of *The Sea Wolf* with his friend George Sterling who was to see it through the press.

The voyage was ill-fated from the start. While still on board ship, Jack came down with the grippe and, on top of this, hurt his ankle. Once in Japan he was unable to get to the scene of the actual fighting because of the strict Japanese regulations covering correspondents. Then he was arrested for taking pictures. To elude the censors and get his stories, he hired a native junk to take him to Chemulpo in Chosen (Korea). For six days and nights he was on a tiny boat in freezing weather with only cold native food to subsist on. An English photographer who saw him arrive at Chemulpo reported: "He was a physical wreck. His ears were frozen, his fingers were frozen, his feet were frozen." But, despite his condition, Jack pushed on towards the front, and finally, after weeks of travel through mud and ice, he reached the battle lines at Yalu. He was immediately ordered back and thrown into a military prison. Later he managed to get some dispatches through the censor, but he was convinced that he was a failure as a war correspondent. "Only in another war, with a white man's army may I hope to redeem myself," he wrote as he returned home in disgust.

That a "yellow, inferior race" like the Japanese could defeat the Russians, a white people, drove London frantic and, in his dispatches to the Hearst press, his lamentations came through clearly. In one dispatch which appeared in the *New York American and Journal* of June 12, 1904, he told of his sensations at the sight of a group of Russian prisoners:

> . . . *the sight I saw was a blow in the face to me. On my mind it had all the stunning effect of the sharp impact of a man's fist. There was a man, a white man, with blue eyes, looking at me. He was dirty and unkempt. He had been through a*

*fierce battle. But his eyes were bluer than mine, and his skin
was as white. And there were other white men in there with
him, many white men.*

*I caught myself gasping. A choking sensation was in my
throat. These men were my kind. I found myself suddenly and
sharply aware that I was an alien among the brown men who
peered in through the windows at me. And I felt myself
strangely alone with those other men behind the window, felt
that my place was there inside with them in their captivity
rather than outside in freedom among the aliens.*

All this, of course, was grist to the mills of the Hearst press then
engaged in a campaign against the "Yellow Peril" and for the ex-
clusion of Asiatics from the United States, but the socialists in this
country found London's accounts of his Japanese experiences revolt-
ing. Some of his comrades in Oakland rebuked him for his race
chauvinism which, according to the reminiscences of one of the members of the branch, brought from London the retort: "What the devil!
I am first of all a white man and only then a Socialist."

When Jack returned from Japan, Bessie began divorce proceedings. With the press featuring every detail of his personal affairs, he
settled down at Glen Ellen with his mother, waiting until Bessie's
divorce became final so that he could marry Charmian Kittredge.

While Jack London was returning home from his trip to Japan,
the Socialist Party met in Chicago and nominated Eugene V. Debs
and Ben Hanford for President and Vice President of the United
States. The Party platform defined socialism as meaning that "all
those things upon which the people in common depend shall by the
people in common be owned and administered; that all production
shall be for the direct use of the producers." For its immediate program the Party pledged itself to work for shorter working days and
higher wages; for the insurance of the workers against accident, sick-
ness and lack of employment; for pensions for aged and exhausted
workers; for the public ownership of the means of transportation,
communication and exchange; for the graduated taxation of incomes,
inheritances, franchises and land values; for the complete education of
children and the complete abolition of child labor.

The press ignored both the socialist candidates and platform until
the Democratic party rejected William Jennings Bryan as being too
radical, and in his stead nominated Judge Alton B. Parker of New

York on a conservative gold-standard platform. The action immediately put life into the socialist campaign, for it was obvious that many voters, convinced that there was no difference between the major parties, would be looking for a new avenue to express their discontent. Debs issued a statement reminding "Democrats, progressives, liberals, humanitarians; you now have no place to go except the Socialist Party."

But not even the most enthusiastic socialist was prepared for the outcome of the election. Debs and Hanford gained almost a half million votes; in California alone the vote for the socialist candidates rose from 7,572 in 1900 to over 35,000 in 1904. The old-line politicians were simply astounded, and all over the country newspapers and magazines began to probe into the reasons for this astounding rise in the socialist vote. The *San Francisco Examiner* called on Jack London, whom it described as "one of the World's greatest authorities on Socialism," for an explanation.

In his article London did not content himself with analyzing simply the background of the national campaign of 1904. He told the readers of the Hearst paper that socialism was not confined to one country, but was an international movement which "had fastened upon every civilized country in the world." He quoted from a message sent to the Socialists of Russia by their comrades in Japan assuring them that the war between their two countries was being conducted for imperialist purposes, and which added, "but for us Socialists there are no boundaries, race, country or nationality. We are comrades, brothers and sisters, and have no reason to fight." Socialism, London continued, was destined to grow stronger in the United States, for it was a fundamental movement. Unlike Populism, which was doomed to die quickly because it only scratched the surface of society's evils, Socialism was "a revolutionary movement that aims to pull down society to its foundations and upon a new foundation to build a new society where shall reign order, equity and justice." The history of society, he reminded his readers, was a history of class struggle, and just as the capitalists overthrew the feudal lords so would the working class triumph over their class enemies: "That the working class shall conquer (mark the note of fatalism) is as certain as the rising of the sun."

London, of course, was letting his imagination run riot when he told the readers of the *Examiner* that the vote cast for Debs "was the tally of the American citizens who have raised the red banner of revolt."

The majority of these voters were simply voicing their dissatisfaction over the control of both major parties by big business and were more concerned with some of the immediate demands of the Socialist Party than with its ultimate goal. Still London's explanation of the great socialist vote in 1904 brought home to a large body of the American people that they were dealing with a world-wide phenomenon, a truly fundamental movement, and not a flash-in-the-pan. Furthermore, it is highly significant that London wrote so glowingly of the Japanese socialists and of their pronouncement that "for us Socialists there are no boundaries, race, country or nationality." Here again, when writing about the Cause that was so close to his heart, Marx and Engels rather than Nietzsche, Spencer, Kidd and Haeckel dominated his thinking.

Jack London was now a famous writer. *The Call of the Wild* had established his popularity, and his dispatches from Japan, headlined as they were in the Hearst newspaper chain, had made his name familiar to millions of Americans who did not usually read books. It is hardly surprising, then, that when *The Sea Wolf* was announced for publication, the advance sales totaled 40,000 copies before the book was off the press. It hit the best-sellers' list the moment it appeared in November, 1904. Critical acclaim was instant. Some reviewers found it a disgusting book, but the majority agreed that it was a work of "rare and original genius." Perhaps the most penetrating comment came from Ambrose Bierce, a fellow Californian, who wrote to George Sterling on February 18, 1905:

> *Yes, you sent me "The Sea Wolf." My opinion of it? Certainly—or a part of it. It is a most disagreeable book, as a whole. London has a pretty bad style and no sense of proportion. The story is a perfect welter of disagreeable incidents. Two or three (of the kind) would have sufficed to show the character of the man Larsen; and his own self-revelings by word of mouth would have "done the rest." Many of these incidents, too, are impossible—such as that of a man mounting a ladder with a dozen other men—more or less—hanging to his leg, and the hero's work of rerigging a wreck and getting it off a beach where it had stuck for weeks, and so forth. The "love" element, with its absurd suppressions and impossible proprieties, is awful. I confess to an overwhelming contempt for both sexless lovers.*

> *Now as to the merits. It is a rattling good story in one way;*
> *something is "going on" all the time—not always what one*
> *would wish, but something. One does not go to sleep over the*
> *book. But the great thing—and it is among the greatest of*
> *things—is that tremendous creation, Wolf Larsen. If that is*
> *not a permanent addition to literature, it is at least a permanent*
> *figure in the memory of the reader. You "can't lose" Wolf Lar-*
> *sen. He will be with you to the end. So it does not really matter*
> *how London has hammered him into you. You may quarrel*
> *with the methods, but the result is almost incomparable. The*
> *hewing out and setting up of such a figure is enough for a man*
> *to do in one life-time. I have hardly words to impart my good*
> *judgment of that work.*

Just what did London have in mind in creating that remarkable character, Wolf Larsen? All of the critics saw in him the glorification of the Nietzschean superman, and, at first glance, it is not difficult to understand why. Wolf Larsen, captain of the *Ghost,* is a perfect Nietzschean speciman, a man with a splendid body and a splendid mind. He can jump six feet across the deck and land a fist into a deck hand's body so that the deck hand will be lifted off his feet. He can strangle a bull-necked mate as easily as wringing a floor mop. He can squeeze a potato, and it will squirt "out between his fingers in streams." He can brush his chief mate away with a back-handed sweep of the arm, gentle enough, apparently, "but which hurls Johansen back like a cork, driving his head against the well with a crash." Yet he is also a philosopher. He has read Darwin and Spencer; he quotes Browning, reads Ecclesiastes, and his shelves of books include Tennyson, Poe, DeQuincey and other classics. He spends hours in interminable discussions with Maud Brewster and Humphrey Van Weyden, and nothing these two highly educated people say can confound him. He holds his own in both worlds—the physical and the intellectual.

Yet a careful reading of the book reveals that behind the exciting outward story is a message which none of the critics grasped—that under the present system the individualist must end in self-destruction. Torn by inner contradictions, unable to solve his own problems, Wolf Larsen became bitter, warped and vicious, a fiend who sadistically persecutes others. In the end the superman collapses, paralyzed and rendered impotent by one of his recurring headaches, his giant body and will of steel eaten away. His brutality, his ruthlessness are a mask for his inner weakness and fear. His ultimate self-destruction is a logical result of the failure of individualism.

This then, London stoutly maintained, was the message of *The Sea Wolf*. In 1915, a year before his death, he wrote to Mary Austin: ". . . Long years ago, at the very beginning of my writing career, I attacked Nietzsche and his super-man idea. This was in *The Sea Wolf*. Lots of people read *The Sea Wolf*, no one discovered that it was an attack upon the super-man philosophy." One can, of course, argue that it was London's duty so to present his message that it could not possibly be misinterpreted, yet it is significant that in many of the comments on London's writings which appeared after his death, the writers declared that, upon second reading, they found no difficulty in discerning London's social message in *The Sea Wolf*.

The years 1905–1907 marked the period of Jack London's greatest activity for the socialist movement. During these years he lectured frequently to socialist organizations, toured the East for the Inter-collegiate Socialist Society, raised money for the movement and for various labor causes, wrote numerous essays and stories in which he brought the socialist message before the American reading public, and completed his most important contribution to the literature of socialism, *The Iron Heel*. Just how much all of this added up to as positive gains for the movement was a subject of debate among socialists; one group contended that through London's writings and speeches many Americans received their first introduction to socialism and became inspired converts; another group maintained that his unorthodox and outlandish conduct and flamboyant utterances antagonized respectable people, gave them an erroneous conception of the socialist movement, and that consequently he was more of a detriment than a benefit to the Cause.

There is some truth in both contentions, but in the main London, during these years, gave the socialist movement a needed stimulus. Much of the literature of the American socialist movement was either a curious mixture of reform, revolution and Christian socialism or dull translations of often tedious writings by European theoreticians. (The writings of Lenin, however, appeared not at all in the socialist literature of the period.) London supplied the movement with literature which was alive and vigorous; which applied Marxist theory to the American scene and explained socialism in terms which workers could read without the need of a dictionary to explain the meaning of words far removed from their everyday life. Even conservative critics admitted that London's socialist essays were written in such a "forcible and striking style" as to hold the attention even "of thousands who hate and fear his 'views'." Thus *Bookman* pointed out in its comments on *The War of the Classes,* a collection of London's socialist essays published in April, 1905: ". . . Certainly no other American writer, and probably no English writer, has produced something that can compare with it in forcefulness and literary merit."

But the American socialist movement was in need of what London had to say as well as how he said it. As the election returns in 1904 indicated, the influence of the Socialist Party was growing. No longer isolated from the main body of the American people by De Leon's opposition to immediate demands, the socialists were able to attract many in the countryside and the industrial cities who were losing faith in the major political parties, and who found in the platform of the Socialist Party demands similar to those which had brought them into the Populist movement. In Eugene V. Debs, moreover, the Socialist Party had a leader whose magnetic personality, brilliant oratory and tireless energy captured the hearts of thousands of workers and farmers. Finally, for the first time in American history, the socialists were moving outside the ranks of the foreign-born and appealing to the native-born. As early as December 9, 1902 the *Milwaukee Daily News,* a Democratic newspaper, declared:

> *The assumption that the Socialist party appeals alone to the foreign born voters is hardly borne out by the election returns, although it is quite true that until recently the socialist propaganda in the United States has been carried on largely by German Socialists. Since the party has taken the aggressive and occupied the field left vacant by the Populist party, it has drawn within its membership all classes and conditions of men—one of its most conspicuous champions being a millionaire and a Harvard graduate.*

Unwittingly, however, this same observation touched upon a major weakness in the Socialist Party which was to grow in importance as the years went by and to overshadow many of its positive contributions. The Party grew rapidly, running up its membership from a few thousand in 1901 to 42,000 in 1909 and to 118,000 in 1912, at the same time increasing its vote in national elections from 87,000 in 1900 to close to a million in 1912. The socialist movement was running at flood tide, but a considerable portion of the new membership came from outside the working-class—lawyers, doctors, dentists, preachers, educators, small manufacturers and business men and an occasional millionaire. Being persuasive speakers and excellent parliamentarians they quickly rose to leadership in the Party and came to control its policies, pushing the working-class members into the background. As one socialist put it, they were "soft and shifty stuff for Socialism to build on." Most of them knew little of Marxism, looked with horror upon revolutionary agitation among the masses, believed that with the capture of sufficient political offices through the ballot box socialism could rapidly be achieved, and preached an emotional propaganda filled with Christian ethics but ignoring the class-struggle.

It was in combating these reformist influences in the Socialist Party that Jack London was to make his greatest contributions as a writer and speaker. The strength, vigor, militant fire and forthright and fearless character of his speeches and writings were in sharp contrast to the propaganda spread by the middle-class intellectuals in the Party. As the *International Socialist Review*, organ of the left-wing elements in the Party, pointed out in discussing *The War of the Classes*:

> . . . *The trouble with London is that he is not the ordinary kind of a literary socialist. It would be easy to name a half dozen prominent writers of the last decade who have occasionally admitted that they were socialists, but their socialism was generally of such a mild inoffensive sort that it didn't hurt them much with their capitalist friends. London, however, is the genuine, old-fashioned, proletarian, class-struggle socialist. His socialism is like everything else about him, virile, combative and genuine to the backbone.*

Almost from the beginning of his career as a socialist, Jack London had seen the danger of the domination of the movement by the middle class intellectuals and had sought to identify himself closely with the working class. This he continued to do during the period of his greatest activity in the movement. In an address at a socialist meeting in Los Angeles in 1905, he repudiated the chairman's characterization of him as "a ripe scholar, a profound philosopher, a literary genius and the foremost man of letters in America," and said: "Before people had given me any of these titles with which the chairman so lavishly credits me, I was working in a cannery, a pickle factory,

was a sailor before the mast, and spent months at a time looking for
work in the ranks of the unemployed; and it is the proletarian side
of my life that I revere the most, and to which I will cling as long as
I live."

The amazing success of *The Sea Wolf* brought London requests for
speaking engagements from all sorts of groups. The University of
California invited him to address the student body. He accepted
eagerly. He hated the cloister-like, ivory-tower atmosphere in which
the students prepared for life, and was determined to hit them "a
stinging blow, right between the eyes, and shake their mental processes
a bit, even if I incurred the risk of being called a long-haired anarchist." So on January 20, 1905 he spoke to 3,500 people, most of
them students, with President Wheeler in the chair. Instead of a dis-
course on literature he addressed the students and professors on "The
Revolutionary Spirit of the American Proletariat," opening his speech
with the words that were soon to ring throughout the country:

> *Yesterday morning I received a letter from a man in Arizona.
> It began, "Dear Comrade," and ended "Yours for the Revolu-
> tion." I answered that letter this morning. I began, "Dear
> Comrade," and I ended, "Yours for the Revolution."*
>
> *There are 500,000 men in the United States beginning and
> ending their letters as our letters were begun and ended. There
> are 1,000,000 men in France, 3,000,000 men in Germany, and
> 6,000,000 men in the world beginning and ending their letters
> as ours were begun and ended.*
>
> *Now what do these facts mean? They mean that the Revolu-
> tion is here, now. We are in it. It goes on every day. No man
> can escape it. Oh, it is great! There has been nothing like it
> in the world. Its battle cry is: "Workingmen of the world,
> unite. You have nothing to lose but your chains. You have
> a world to gain." Our Revolution was a merely local thing
> compared with it. The English revolution was a merely local
> thing compared to it. And so was the French Revolution. This
> Revolution is as wide as the earth. Its men clasp hands around
> the globe. The Japanese Socialist hails the Russian Socialist,
> and the German Socialist hails the French Socialist with the
> same word that we California Socialists hail each other, the
> noble word, COMRADE.*

Why were these men socialists, London asked? What was it that drove them "unceasingly to work for the Revolution, to go to prison for it, to go into exile for it, to die for it?" He told the students and professors of his experiences in the London slums when he was writing *The People of the Abyss*, reminding them that in the British capital alone, close to two million people lived on the poverty line and below it and another million "with one week's wages between them and pauperism," while in all of Europe sixty million people suffered from hunger and want. He quoted from the English scholar, Frederick W. Harrison who, after studying the condition of the poor in Europe, had concluded: "If this is to be the permanent condition of modern society, civilization must be held to bring a curse on the great majority of mankind." Then he urged his audience to read Robert Hunter's *Poverty*, a detailed study of social conditions in the United States and he quoted statistics from the book which had just been published by Macmillan, which proved that even in fairly prosperous years there were no less than ten million persons in this country who were "underfed, underclothed and poorly housed," that over a million and a half little children "were forced to become wage earners when they should still be in school," that about five million women found it necessary to work, that no less than one million workers were injured or killed each year while at work, and about ten million persons "now living, will, if the present ratio be kept up, die of the preventable disease, tuberculosis."

It was such facts, said London, and "the glorious ideas of Socialism" that kept the revolutionists unceasingly at work and it was this, too, that had convinced him "that the capitalist system which has so grossly and criminally mismanaged our industrial life must be swept away, and the Socialist system put in its place." He told them frankly what the socialists were striving to achieve: "We propose to destroy present-day civilization, that is, capitalist civilization, with its brutal struggle of man with man for life—by the ballot, where it is free, be it forever remembered—and replace it by a better civilization, a civilization whose principle shall be 'Each for all and all for Each.'"

London concluded his address with a direct appeal to the University students:

> *As I look over the universities of my land today, I see the students asleep, asleep in the face of the awful facts I have given you, asleep in the greatest revolution that has ever come*

> *to the world. Oh, it is sad! Not long ago, revolutions began,*
> *grew, broke out, in Oxford. Today Russian universities seethe*
> *with revolution. I say to you, then: University men and women,*
> *you men and women in the full glory of life, here is a cause*
> *that appeals to all the romance in you. Awake to its call. Line*
> *up! Line up! All the world despises a coward. Read our books.*
> *Fight us, if you do not agree with us. But by all that is brave*
> *and strong, show your colors! Line up! Line up! I say.*

London let his imagination soar when he said that there were six million revolutionists in 1905 who closed their letters, "Yours for the Revolution." But the bulk of the lecture was a carefully-documented and vigorous indictment of capitalism, and it received wide publicity in such socialist journals as the *Socialist Voice* of Oakland and the *Appeal to Reason.*

A few days after his speech at the University of California there came news of Bloody Sunday in St. Petersburg initiating the brutal suppression of the revolutionary movement in Russia. London immediately announced his support of the Russian revolutionists and joined with other leading comrades in issuing a call to the American socialists to raise funds for the Russian revolution. This action, however, received little notice outside of the socialist press. Then London spoke before a businessmen's club in Stockton and, in the course of his remarks, proclaimed that the Russian revolutionists who had assassinated several tsarist officials were his brothers. Immediately the newspaper headlines throughout the country screamed: "Jack London calls Russian Assassins his Brothers," and a clamor arose demanding that he retract his statement, some newspapers even threatening prosecution for treason unless he did so. But London stood firm. He knew that the Russian Revolution of 1905 was an uprising of the working class against capitalist oppression and Tsarist tyranny and that under such an autocratic government it was inevitable that blood would flow when the exploited masses rose up to overthrow their oppressors. As a revolutionary socialist, an internationalist, he acknowledged his comradeship with the Russian revolutionists. The shrieks of the bourgeois press did not move him.

The furore over his remarks before the Stockton businessmen was no sooner off the front pages when he spoke again, quoted William Lloyd Garrison, the great Abolitionist leader, as saying "To Hell with the Constitution" when that document was utilized to defend slavery, and pointed out that General Sherman Bell had said the same thing in 1904 while helping to break the strike of ore miners in Cripple Creek, Colorado. The press deliberately misquoted London; the headlines this time screaming, "Jack London says to Hell with the Constitution." It was useless for him to try to explain that he was not the one who had made the remark; the editorials continued to describe him as a wild-eyed fanatic bent on undermining the most sacred institution in the United States.

These attacks had their effect on public opinion in California, for when London ran again for Mayor of Oakland on the Socialist ticket in the spring of 1905, he received only 981 votes. This was four times his previous total, but it was hardly an impressive showing.

In the summer of 1905 Jack London wrote gleefully to George Bamford from his Hill Ranch near Glen Ellen in Sonoma County which he had just built with his royalties from *The Sea Wolf:* "Oh, take my word, there is no place like the country." A few months later he was crossing the country to conduct a lecture tour for the socialist cause in behalf of the Intercollegiate Socialist Society.

Inspired by the growth in the socialist vote in the 1904 presidential election and by the world-wide repercussions of the Russian Revolution of 1905, a movement got under way to inculcate among college men and women an understanding of socialism. The idea was first advanced by Upton Sinclair, a young Baltimorean who had gone through the College of the City of New York without learning that there was such a thing as a Socialist Party in the United States. This state of affairs, he believed, should be remedied, and college students be made aware of "this mighty new current in modern life." After some discussion with his friend, George Stroebel, it was decided to contact well-known writers and educators to sponsor the organization. Jack London was among the first to be contacted. He expressed immediate interest, agreed to serve as a sponsor, and signed the call announcing the formation of The Intercollegiate Socialist Society:

> *In the opinion of the undersigned* [went the call] *the recent remarkable increase in the Socialist vote in America should serve as an indication to the educated men and women in the country that Socialism is a thing concerning which it is no longer wise to be indifferent.*
>
> *The undersigned, regarding its aims and fundamental prin-*

ciples with sympathy, and believing that in them will ultimately be found the remedy for the far-reaching economic evils, propose organizing an association to be known as the Intercollegiate Socialist Society, for the purpose of promoting an intelligent interest among college men and women, graduate and undergraduate, through the formation of study groups in the colleges and universities, and the encouraging of all legitimate endeavors to awaken an interest in Socialism among the educated men and women of the country.

The undersigned were William English Walling, graduate of the University of Chicago, Thomas Wentworth Higginson, famous Boston author and graduate of Harvard, J. Phelps Stokes, a New York millionaire, Charlotte Perkins Gilman, the great-granddaughter of Lyman Beecher, Clarence S. Darrow, already making a reputation for himself in law, B. O. Flower, the publisher of *The Arena,* Oscar Lovell Triggs, Leonard D. Abbott, Jack London and Upton Sinclair.

At a meeting held in New York City on September 12, 1905, the Society was formally established and Jack London, although not present, was unanimously elected president, and Upton Sinclair and J. Phelps Stokes, vice presidents. Jack's comrades were aware that even though he might not be able to devote too much time to the organization, his name had such great publicity value that it would enable the Society to secure entry into places which otherwise might close its doors upon anything labeled socialist.

Along with Eugene Debs, Charles Edward Russell, Sinclair, Walling, Stokes, and Higginson, London was asked to undertake a lecture tour for the new organization, appearing at colleges, forums or on any other available platform. He accepted, planning to couple his free lectures for the society with talks before women's clubs and businessmen's associations where he would receive the handsome fees he needed for land improvements on his ranch, the upkeep of his family, contributions to the Party, strike funds and labor defense funds, and the building of the *Snark* with which he intended to sail around the world. He started east on a Pullman, accompanied by a Korean valet.

From beginning to end the lecture tour was conducted in a blaze of publicity. He was already one of the most romantic figures of the period, personifying youth and courage, adventure, the sea, the Klondike and the road, and everyone knew that despite his handsome earnings as a writer he was a champion of the underdog. People flocked to hear him and the youth of the country in white shirts with soft collars, tried to look like Jack London and to speak like his characters.

The unfavorable publicity, however, started early in the tour. His divorce became final on November 18, 1905. The next day in Chicago he married Charmian Kittredge only to find that the state law forbade the marriage for a year. When Jack learned of this, he told reporters: "I will get married in every State in the Union just as fast as I can— from one to another, if it is necessary." It was generally agreed that his haste in marrying Charmian was unseemly and this statement brought down upon London a deluge of criticism. In a sermon in Des Moines, Iowa, Dr. James A. Beebe attacked the Women's Club of the city for having invited London to lecture before them and fawning over a person who had "so lightly treated the marriage relation." "To lionize one who is guilty of moral laxity," he declared, "is to condone the offence." Although a number of women's clubs cancelled engagements and some socialists criticized him because the press was putting the blame for his "immorality" on his socialist views, London remained unperturbed. How he conducted his personal life, he asserted, was nobody's business but his own.

Some women's clubs may have been too shocked to hear London lecture, but whenever he spoke at a college or university he addressed capacity audiences. At Harvard two thousand university men—"the pick and flower of perhaps the most luxurious bourgeois society in the world"—packed the great room of the Union. Many were probably more amused than impressed, but London let them have it straight from the shoulder. Again he defended the Russian Revolutionists: "I speak and think of these 'assassins' in Russia as my comrades. So do all the comrades in America, and all the seven million comrades in the world. This is shown by the fact that we do back up all the comrades in Russia. They are not disciples of Tolstoy, nor are we. We are revolutionists."

From Harvard London went to New York where he addressed an exclusive group of extremely wealthy men and women. He was to use the incident several months later in the brilliant chapter of *The Iron Heel*, "The Philomaths." According to an account by Joshua Wanhope who attended the lecture to the wealthy New Yorkers, London concluded his speech with a vehement attack upon the audience:

> *You have been entrusted with the world; you have muddled and mismanaged it. You are incompetent, despite all your*

boastings. A million years ago the caveman, without tools, with small brain, and with nothing but the strength of his body, managed to feed his wife and children, so that through him the race survived. You, on the other hand, armed with all the modern means of production, multiplying the productive capacity of the cavemen a million times—you are incompetents and muddlers, you are unable to secure to millions even the paltry amount of bread that would sustain their physical life. You have mismanaged the world, and it shall be taken from you.

The "silk-stockinged audience," Wanhope recalled "murmured their perturbation, anger and impatience, but the unrelenting London went on":

Who will take it from you? We will! And who are we? We are seven million socialist revolutionists and we are everywhere growing. And we want all you have! Look at us! We are strong! Consider our hands! They are strong hands, and even now they are reaching forth for all you have, and they will take it, take it by the power of their strong hands; take it from your feeble grasp. Long or short though the time may be, that time is coming. The army is on the march, and nothing can stop it, that you can stop it is ludicrous. It wants nothing less than all you have, and it will take it; you are incompetent and will have to surrender to the strong. We are the strong, and in that day we shall give you an exhibition of power such as your feeble brains never dreamed the world contained!

"There was a loud murmur of protest and dissent," Wanhope continued, "and one or two respectable-looking persons choked up, and it seemed as if they were about to have apoplexy. London walked down from the rostrum through a sea of blasted, purple faces distorted with rage, but no attempt was made to detain him. . . . It was not until he was well out of earshot that some of the stunned audience plucked up enough courage to remark that 'he ought to be in jail.' "

Jack was gleeful. He wrote to Bamford: "Oh, I have some stories to tell you when I get back about my clashes with the masters of society!"

On January 26, 1906 London interrupted his stay in New York and went down to New Haven for a lecture at Yale. Dr. Alexander Irvine, minister of the Pilgrim Church in New Haven and secretary of the local Socialist Party, had persuaded the Yale Union, a debating society, to sponsor the lecture on condition that London would stay away from radical topics. Woolsey Hall was rented for the occasion, leaflets were distributed in factories and shops, and posters were plastered over the campus announcing the lecture. The New Haven comrade who had painted the poster showed London in a red turtle-neck sweater with a mass of flames as the background and con-spicuously featured as the title of the lecture the single word, "REVO-LUTION."

Needless to add, the next morning Yale was shocked. For a time it appeared that London would not be permitted to speak, but William Lyon Phelps, one of the younger professors and already a prominent member of the faculty, squashed the movement to cancel the lecture with the simple query, "Is Yale a monastery?"

Three thousand students, three hundred members of the faculty, and citizens of the community, including a group of workers who came to help out if there should be any trouble, packed Woolsey Hall to hear London speak on "Revolution." This famous lecture was an expansion of the talk on "The Revolutionary Spirit of the American Proletariat," delivered a year before at the University of California. It opened with a dramatic report of the millions enrolled in the army of socialism, and made the point that this international organized movement was unequalled in history. It represented a growing flame of revolt, with its own history and traditions and a vast body of scientific literature. The revolutionists addressed each other as "com-rades"; their red banner symbolized, not incendiarism, but the brotherhood of man, and would eventually destroy all national bound-aries. Wherever the law of the land permitted, the revolutionists fought to destroy the existing capitalist society peaceably, at the ballot-box, but where this was not permitted, and force was used against them, they resorted to force themselves, meeting violence with violence.

This huge revolutionary upsurge, London emphasized, was basically a working-class movement. Middle class and professional men were interested in the struggle to overthrow capitalism, but it was never-theless "a distinctly working-class revolt." The middle class was a perishing class, and only the workers would have the strength to carry through the battle for socialism to victory. "The workers of the world, as a class, are fighting the capitalists of the world, as a class," he told the Yale audience.

Then London analyzed the reason for the existence of this vast socialist army and the necessity for a new social order. The present structure of society, he pointed out, was inadequate to meet the needs of humanity—witness unemployment, low wages and hunger. Even the cave dweller lived in greater security than the hungry and homeless for whom the present social order had so little use. Yet, the most incredible part of it all was that there was absolutely no need for misery and starvation, for the means of production were more than adequate to provide food, shelter and clothing for everyone. Still, because of the mismanagement of the capitalist class, thousands upon thousands went unsheltered, hungry and naked. To buttress his point, London, throughout this section of his lecture, cited newspaper reports, sociological studies and U.S. Bureau of Labor reports.

The capitalists were stupid as well as inefficient, he continued. They believed that they could hold back the rising tide of revolution by using violence against the workers—"bayonets, machine-guns, policemen's clubs, professional strike-breakers, and armed Pinkertons." Yet by such tactics they were automatically converting more and more workers into revolutionists.

The ruling class had failed to run the system properly. It was now the turn of the working class. "The capitalist class has been indicted," London concluded. "It has failed in the management and its management is to be taken away from it. Seven million men of the working-class say that they are going to get the rest of the working-class to join with them and take the management away. The revolution is here, now. Stop it who can."

The lecture is one of London's finest essays, presented in clear, vigorous language, colorful and dramatic from beginning to end, even while massing statistics to prove its thesis. Furthermore, its pointed references to the importance of the working-class in the battle to overthrow capitalism and his observations on the secondary role of middle-class and professional men, were not lost on many members of the Socialist Party. All told, like all of London's socialist essays, it is still fresh and meaningful today more than forty years after it was written.

In the middle of his prepared lecture at Yale, London interpolated a bitter comment on the role of the American colleges and universities:

> *I went to the University. I found the University, in the main,
> practically wholly so, clean and noble, but I did not find the*

university alive. I found that the American university had this ideal, as phrased by a professor in Chicago University [Paul Shorey], namely: "The passionless pursuit of passionless intelligence"—clean and noble, I grant you, but not alive enough. . . . And the reflection of this university ideal I find— the conservatism and unconcern of the American people toward those who are suffering, who are in want. And so I became interested in an attempt to arouse in the minds of the young men of our universities an interest in the study of socialism. . . . We do not desire merely to make converts. . . . If collegians cannot fight for us, we want them to fight against us— of course, sincerely fight against us. But what we do not want is that which obtains today and has obtained in the past of the university, a mere deadness and unconcern and ignorance so far as socialism is concerned. Fight for us or fight against us! Raise your voices one way or the other; be alive!

When he finished, London received a tremendous ovation from the students and was carried off the platform on the shoulders of a group of Yale men. Even some of the faculty members shared this enthusiasm. "A Professor of Yale," Dr. Irvine once remarked, "told me a few days after the lecture that it was the greatest intellectual stimulus Yale had had in many years, and he sincerely hoped that London would return and expound the same program in the same hall." The press, to say the least, did not echo these sentiments. The New Haven papers were furious that the students had been exposed to the "rantings" of a socialist and the New York papers took up the cry. The *New York Times* devoted a long editorial on February 1, 1906 to London's speech at Yale in which it paid Jack a left-handed compliment, commending him "for the perfect frankness with which he tells his audiences what socialism is, and what it aims to accomplish." Unlike most of his comrades, said the *Times* piously, Jack London "does not croak socialism in timid disguises. He does not profess to regard it as mere return to the principle of the golden rule, or as a reform altogether beneficent that will harm nobody and make all the world happier. Mr. Jack London's Socialism is bloody war—the war of one class in society against other classes. He says so. It is a destructive socialism. He glories in it." Then the *Times* calmly proceeded to distort London's remarks at Yale in the process of which Jack was quoted as saying: "If people object to our programme because of the Constitution, then to hell with the Constitution. Yes, to hell with the Constitution."

> *That is what Socialism means* [the *Times* concluded.] *It is to the accomplishment of these things that Socialism tends. Consciously or unconsciously, pretty much all Socialists want to see Mr. Jack London's reforms achieved, and to see them achieved in Mr. Jack London's way. . . . Very few Socialists, however, have Mr. Jack London's courage. Again we say, he must be commended for his courage and for his honesty. Society can judge Socialism better and reach sounder conclusions upon its merits when it has a correct understanding of the nature of Socialism and the intentions of Socialists.*

London did not bother to answer the *Times*, but Upton Sinclair, in a letter to the editor, sought to correct the "wrong impression" created by the "quotation" from the Yale speech. When London referred to the "blood-red banner" of revolution, wrote Sinclair, he "took pains to explain to the audience that he meant it 'as a symbol of brotherhood of Man, and not of war and destruction' "; when he mentioned the words "to hell with the Constitution," he was referring to the remarks of "a militia General who at one time held sway in the State of Colorado," and when he talked of wresting power from the rulers, "by war if necessary," he explained to the audience that "the Socialist Party is a party of Constitutional agitation in countries where universal suffrage and free speech prevail, and that in countries where these Constitutional rights are denied it resorts to force."

Sinclair also took the *Times* to task for implying that most Socialists shrank from stating their aims as courageously and frankly as did Jack London. "I heard Jack London's address," Sinclair wrote sharply. "I have heard and read many other Socialist addresses, and so far as I know there is no such difference to be noted between them."

As Jack could have told him in advance, Sinclair's letter satisfied nobody. The newspapers continued to attribute to London the remark, "To hell with the Constitution," and editorials still persisted in distorting his speeches by quoting excerpts out of context. On February 8, three days after Sinclair's letter appeared in the *Times*, the public library in Derby Neck, Connecticut, withdrew from circulation all of Jack London's works, making the following announcement: "As Jack London publicly announces that he is an anarchist, devoting the Constitution to hell and the government to destruction, we have ordered all of his works withdrawn from circulation, and we urge not only other libraries to do likewise, but all lovers of their country to cease buying his books or taking magazines publishing his stories." Several other libraries responded immediately and all over the country arose the cry, "Boycott all magazines which contain stories by Jack London."

All this was to bring a decided slump in the sales of London's books. But what disturbed Jack much more than this was that it started a wave of consternation among the middle-class leaders of the Socialist Party who became frightened lest London's utterances be taken for the official position of the movement. When Jack quoted with approval Gene Debs' remark, "There is no good capitalist and no bad workingman," and when he talked of the class-struggle, a shudder ran through many right wing socialists. Fearing that the more timid members of the Party and its sympathizers were being antagonized by London's speeches, they were quick to disassociate themselves from his views. When J. G. Phelps Stokes introduced Jack to an audience at the Grand Central Palace in New York, he made it quite clear that he and other socialists did not agree with London that "the catastrophe which these things (the accumulation of wealth and power in the hands of the few, and the like) threaten will necessarily come upon us." The remark did not cause Jack to pull his punches. He was tired from a speaking trip to Florida and back, and was suffering from an attack of tonsilitis. Yet, as Upton Sinclair relates: "Amid the waving of red handkerchiefs, and in a voice of calm defiance he read to the city of New York his stunning 'Revolution'. . . ."

London continued with his lecture tour for the Intercollegiate Socialist Society, but on February 3, 1906 he fell seriously ill in St. Paul. The rest of his tour was cancelled and he returned to Glen Ellen. On February 22, he wrote to Anna Strunsky: "Back again after four months of lecturing. I rattled the dry bones some. Spoke at Yale, Harvard, Columbia, University of Chicago, and a lot of speeches for the Socialist Party." His lectures were never resumed.

While Jack London was by no means the only Socialist to popularize the Cause among college students, he, more than anyone, was the college man's idol and his lectures brought many of them closer to the movement. He himself felt that the work of the Intercollegiate Socialist Society was of great importance and disagreed sharply with those in the Party who believed that the organization should be disbanded. In every college where he lectured, he told George Bamford, he "found a number of socialistically inclined and non-Socialist students earnest and sincere, who were eager to form an Intercollegiate Socialist Society group," and if the Society had not existed nothing could have been accomplished. He admitted that not everyone who joined the Society was a full-fledged Socialist, but he was convinced "that the majority of the members will be hammered into Socialism. . . . In the meantime discussion will take place, reading is done, and the word 'Socialism' becomes a less misunderstood term in such a college."

London's lecture tour was important in still another respect. While most newspapers ignored London's carefully documented indictment of capitalism, concerning themselves with only a few phrases from his speeches which they could quote for their own purposes, a few did make an effort to check up on his facts. Thus when London cited the miserable wages of garment workers in Chicago in the course of his "Revolution" speech, concluding that "such wages means no childhood for the children, beastliness of living, and starvation for all," the *Chicago American* put its reporters to work to investigate the matter, and devoted several pages to their findings. The story opened:

> *Slaves in Chicago—slaves of the sweat shops, toiling all day long and making 15 cents—one family of three which earned a total of $2.50 as a total last week—a strong man who earned 95 cents in the same time—a woman who thinks $1.25 a week is a good wage and who supports two children on 90 cents a week—these were conditions discovered today by reporters for the* Chicago American *investigating the sweat shops of Chicago.*
>
> *Already enough facts have come to light to prove abundantly the assertion of Jack London, novelist and Socialist lecturer in a New York address, that many girls and women in Chicago earn only 90 cents a week.*
>
> *The* Chicago American *has found these statements to be true. There are many women in Chicago who earn no more than 90 cents a week. . . .*

Then followed a series of interviews with Italian garment workers which brought out the full details of the "beastliness" of their living. To London such newspaper articles were more important than the banning of his books by libraries and the boycotting of magazines featuring his stories, for he took pride in the fact that his lectures and essays were carefully documented with evidence secured through an exhaustive source study. The newspapers liked to give the impression that London was simply infatuated with the sound of radical slogans. The truth is that London was a careful student of contemporary society and when he sat down to write a socialist essay or story, he drew on his vast collection of clippings from newspapers, magazines, books and government reports. This material was in turn utilized by socialists and trade unionists in their own talks and writings. "There are enough striking illustrations and strong quotations between the covers of this little book," said the *International Socialist Review* of *The War of the Classes,* "to supply an army of soap box orators with ammunition." London was overjoyed at such use of his material. "I'd rather see every bit of Socialistic work I have done pirated, and given a larger circulation . . . ," he wrote to Fred Bamford on June 26, 1906, "than to receive full credit for it and narrower circulation."

Even after his withdrawal from active work for the Intercollegiate Socialist Society, London was to aid in the growth of the organization through his essay, "What Life Means to Me," written expressly for the Society and published as its first pamphlet. In this essay, probably his finest piece of autobiographical writing, London looks back through the years evaluating his own experiences up to the time that he first gained a true perspective on life—the time that he was able to see what part the philosophy of socialism played in his life. He writes of his beginnings in the working class, and of the inner fire that made him want to climb out of his class where everything seemed so ugly into the ranks of those who wore beautiful clothes and had plenty to eat and whose life was surely pure and noble and clean. But society kept him from moving upwards and he was forced to work at every conceivable job to keep alive. He learned that life was a business of selling that which could make profit for others and he decided to sell brains rather than muscle which wore out too quickly and did not command a sufficiently high price. He came in contact with socialists and, for the first time, life seemed worthwhile. He was among "great souls who exalted flesh and spirit over dollars and cents, and to whom the thin wail of the starved slum child meant more than all the pomp and circumstance of commercial expansion and world empire." Finally, as a "brain merchant" he climbed out of the pit, and found that those on the top of the ladder were clean and beautiful, but that about them was an air of hypocrisy that nauseated him. And above all he found that they were not alive; that they had nothing to offer him. So he returned to his comrades, content to work with them for the Revolution. Looking forward to that day, he predicts: "Then we'll cleanse the cellar and build a new habitation for mankind, in which there will be no parlor floor, in which all the rooms will be bright and airy, and where the air that is breathed will be clean, noble, and alive." He concludes with a reaffirmation of his faith in the inevitable triumph of socialism:

> *And last of all, my faith is in the working-class. As some Frenchman has said, "The stairway of time is ever echoing with the wooden shoe going up, the polished boot descending."*

In June the keel of the *Snark* was laid while London was busy at work on *The Iron Heel* and while he was contacting editors for the publication rights of stories and articles arising from his projected voyage to the South Seas. But he also took time off to write a review of Upton Sinclair's great muckraking novel of conditions in the Chicago meat-packing industry, *The Jungle*.

When the *Appeal to Reason*, late in 1905, serialized Sinclair's novel, London immediately expressed his enthusiasm for the work. "It has stirred me," he wrote to the author, "and made me sit right up time and again. There has been nothing done like it. You have my heartiest congratulations." A little later when Sinclair, who had found it impossible to secure a publisher and had decided to publish the book himself, appealed to London for aid, Jack responded with a resounding call to the readers of the *Appeal to Reason* urging them to send in advance orders to make possible the publication of the book. This call, published in the November 18, 1905 issue of the *Appeal to Reason*, is so full of London's enthusiasm that it merits quotation in full:

> *Dear Comrades:*
>
> *Here it is at last! The book we have been waiting for these many years! The "Uncle Tom's Cabin" of wage slavery! Comrade Sinclair's book, "The Jungle!" and what "Uncle Tom's Cabin" did for black slaves, "The Jungle" has a large chance to do for the wage-slaves of today.*
>
> *It is essentially a book of today. The beautiful theoretics of Bellamy's "Looking Backward" are all very good. They served a purpose, and served it well. "Looking Backward" was a great book. But I dare say that "The Jungle," which has no beautiful theoretics, is even a greater book.*

It is alive and warm. It is brutal with life. It is written of sweat and blood, and groans and tears. It depicts, not what man ought to be, but what man is compelled to be in our world, in the Twentieth Century. It depicts, not what our country ought to be, or what it seems to be in the fancies of Fourth of July spell-binders, the home of liberty and equality of opportunity; but it depicts what our country really is, the home of oppression and injustice, a nightmare of misery, an inferno of suffering, a human hell, a jungle of wild beasts.

And there you have the very essence of Comrade Sinclair's book—the jungle! And that is what he has named it. This book must go. And you, comrades, must make it go. It is a labor of love on the part of the man who wrote it. It must be a labor of love on your part to distribute it.

And take notice and remember, comrades, this book is straight proletarian. And straight proletarian it must be throughout. It is written by an intellectual proletarian. It is written for the proletarian. It is to be published by a proletarian publishing house. It is to be read by the proletariat. And depend upon it, if it is not circulated by the proletariat it will not be circulated at all. In short, it must be a supreme proletarian effort.

Remember, this book must go out in the face of the enemy. No capitalist publishing house would dare to publish it. It will be laughed at—some; jeered at—some; abused some; but most of all, worst of all, the most dangerous treatment it will receive is that of silence. For that is the way of capitalism.

Comrades, do not forget the conspiracy of silence. Silence is the deadliest danger this book has to face. The book stands on its own merits. You have read it, and you know. All that it requires is a hearing. This hearing you must get for it. You must not permit this silence. You must shout out this book from the housetops; at all times, and at all places. You must talk about it, howl about it, do everything but keep quiet about it. Open your mouths and let out your lungs, raise such a clamor that those in the high places will wonder what all the row is about and perchance feel tottering under them the edifices of greed they have reared.

All you have to do is to give this book a start. You have read the book yourselves, and you will vouch for it. Once it gets

> its start it will run away from you. The printers will be worked
> to death getting out larger and larger editions. It will go out
> by the hundreds of thousands. It will be read by every work-
> ingman. It will open countless ears that have been deaf to
> Socialism. It will plough the soil for the seed of our propa-
> ganda. It will wake thousands of converts to our cause. Com-
> rades, it is up to you!
>
> > *Yours for the Revolution,*
> > *Jack London.*

Within a short time after this appeal was published, five thousand
advance orders (with funds enclosed) were received. The book was
published by the Jungle Publishing Company. Soon afterwards,
Doubleday, Page and Company, in spite of threats of law suits, decided to put it out under its imprint. As soon as the book appeared,
London wrote a glowing review for the Hearst papers, an emasculated
version of which was finally published in the *New York Journal* of
August 8, 1906. Furious at the censorship imposed upon him, London
sent the review to *Wilshire's Magazine* which printed it a month later
with the following editorial note appended:

> *The full text of this remarkable review of the "Jungle" has
> never before been published. It was originally sent by the re-
> viewer to the Hearst papers and after lying unused for several
> months was finally printed in an abbreviated and mutilated
> condition, or, as the virile London says, "with the guts taken
> out of it." Mr. London forwarded the review to this office, leav-
> ing it to us as to whether it should be published or not. We
> believe that our readers will be interested in this powerful
> synopsis of Sinclair's famous book, even if it is a trifle belated,
> and it is therefore reproduced here.*

The Jungle rapidly became a best-seller, caused a nationwide furore
and brought about a Congressional investigation of the packing houses
of Chicago, yet it was London's enthusiastic support that started it
on its way to success. "If that book went all over the world," Sinclair
himself admitted, "it was Jack London's push that started it."

There were many sequels to London's action in the case of *The
Jungle,* and all so characteristic of him that they always remained in
the minds of those who knew him intimately as among the really
beautiful things in his life. "As I watched him, through the eleven

years that passed after that," wrote Upton Sinclair a year after London's death, "I saw that that action was not a single impulse, but an expression of his deepest nature. He was open-handedness incarnate; save only to editors and publishers whom he hated—on principle, be it said, as part of the class struggle! Towards young writers he was as a mother to a brood of children; perhaps he over-fed some of them with his praise. I know it was not enough to write of his pleasure in a note in the case of Lawrence's *Sons and Lovers,* his eager haste required a telegram! He knew all about the uphill fight a young radical had to make, and to such he gave both praise and money for the helping of the glorious cause. That is the thing for which I loved him most; I have saved it to the last, so that it may be the thing the reader carries away with him—the memory of a man strong, yet tender-hearted as a child, honest and open as daylight, generous as Mother Nature herself."

All this while, the *Snark* was costing London every penny he earned by his writings. So he wrote anything he could think of that would sell and furnish the money to pour into his boat. He was up to his neck in work. "Say," he wrote to Gaylord Wilshire on August 27, 1906, in answer to a request for an article, "if you had asked me for my wife or for my ranch, it would have been easier for me to have given them to you than for me to give you that article. I am so absolutely rushed to death with my work (writing), and with the stupendous volume of details of finishing building the boat and preparing for departure, that I cannot even *think* of what to write in such an article, must less find the *time,* in which to write it. Think! Why, all I can think about these days is how to make sea-anchors and oil-drags; how to make ice; how to make electricity; how to make gasoline engines go; how to store 1,000 gallons of gasoline on a small boat where there isn't room for 500 gallons. How to navigate— my God, man, do you realize that in a few short weeks we set sail, and I haven't had a bit of time in which to learn navigation? Time! If you can see any way to manage it, I'd sooner you sent me 200 hours of time than $200."

Jack was over-optimistic when he spoke of a few weeks; it was not to be until April 23 of the following year that he set sail out of the Golden Gate. During these months he kept writing and writing, to meet the mounting costs of his boat. The books and stories poured out one after another—*Moon-Face and other stories,* an unimportant collection, September, 1906; *White Fang,* a novel about a dog, half-wolf, who through mistreatment becomes savage and through love and kindness, becomes docile and loyal, September, 1906; *Scorn of Women,* a play, November, 1906; *Before Adam,* a thrilling novel of primitive life using an interesting dream device, February, 1907, and numerous other short stories and articles including the series on his tramping experiences in *Cosmopolitan Magazine* in 1907 under the title "My Life in the Underworld" and published by Macmillan in November, 1907 as *The Road.*

Pressed as he was to raise the thirty thousand dollars that went into the building of the *Snark,* London's interest in the struggles of the working-class remained undiminished. Three of his finest contributions to the literature of the radical movement were written during this harassing period: "The Apostate," "Something Rotten in Idaho," and *The Iron Heel.*

London had been asked by an influential magazine to investigate and write on conditions of child-labor in Southern cotton mills, but bent on finishing *The Iron Heel* and tossing off material that would raise money quickly, he had rejected the tempting offer. Still he could not forget his own boyhood experiences in the jute mill, cannery and laundry and, putting other work aside, he wrote a tale of uncompromising realism dealing with child labor, "The Apostate," which appeared in *Woman's Home Companion* in September, 1906 and became one of the most popular of the socialist pamphlets.

The title character is a boy of about seventeen, a bobbin winder in a jute mill, stunted, a work-slave since the age of seven. The story opens in the bedroom of a ramshackle home with the mother shaking the boy to wake him up before dawn of a cold day, the boy fighting for sleep and his mother warning him, "You'll be docked." Only a writer who had gone through such experiences himself could convey such a realistic picture of the boy's utter weariness. Equally effective is the picture of the poverty-stricken home—the chill of the room, the malodorous sink, the wretched coffee, the careful doling out of the scanty food. As the five-thirty whistle blows, the scene shifts to the mill. Here one meets the other children, some crippled, all undernourished and rickety and each with the inevitable hacking cough from the lint. Here too is the harsh overseer, the superintendent who allows himself to be deceived by the boys' ages. Johnny (the apostate-to-be) is the star-worker, self-trained by years of monotonous work.

Morning after morning Johnny is "torn bodily by his mother from the grip of sleep." At last, when he is about sixteen, comes illness and a long convalescence. He sleeps and sleeps, and thinks. When well, he announces simply but irrevocably, that he will work no more. Despite his mother's tears, he walks out of the city, towards the open country. "He did not walk like a man," London writes. "He did not look like a man. He was a travesty of the human. It was a twisted and stunted and nameless piece of life that shambled like a sickly ape, arms loose-hanging, stoop-shouldered, narrow-chested, grotesque and terrible."

"Something Rotten in Idaho" grew out of the famous Moyer-Haywood-Pettibone case. The climax of years of class struggle in Idaho between the Western Federation of Miners and the corporations came on December 30, 1905 when former Governor Steunenberg, who had been responsible for much anti-labor violence during his administration, was assassinated by the explosion of a bomb attached to the gate of his ranch. The man who set the bomb, Harry Orchard, had a long criminal record; he was arrested, held incommunicado in jail, and then turned over to the Pinkerton Agency, which specialized in providing strike breakers and company police. Through a deal Orchard made with the Pinkertons, Charles Moyer, William "Big Bill" Haywood and George Pettibone, officers of the Western Federation of Miners, were arrested in Denver, kidnapped by the police of Idaho without extradition papers, locked in the state penitentiary in Boise, and charged with conspiracy to murder ex-Governor Steunenberg. All this, it soon became clear, had been secretly arranged by the Governors of Colorado and Idaho in collusion with the mining corporations.

Immediately the socialist and labor movements sprang to the defense of the three men, realizing that the blow was actually directed against the militant industrial union they led. Eugene V. Debs wrote a stirring call to action in the *Appeal to Reason:*

AROUSE YE SLAVES!

> *Murder has been plotted and is about to be executed in the name and under the form of law. Charles Moyer and William D. Haywood, of the Western Federation of Miners, are charged with the assassination of ex-Governor Frank Steunenberg, of Idaho, as a mere subterfuge to pounce upon them in secret, rush them out of the state by special train, clap them in the penitentiary, convict them upon the purchased, perjured testimony of villains, and then strangle them to death with the hangman's noose. If they attempt to murder Moyer, Haywood*

and their brothers, a million revolutionists will meet them with guns.

President Theodore Roosevelt called Debs, Moyer and Haywood undesirable citizens, but the movement in behalf of the three men grew. Habeas corpus proceedings were started before a Federal District Court judge, and when the writ was denied, an appeal was taken to the Supreme Court. But the highest judicial tribunal evaded the appeal by taking a long summer vacation. Meanwhile, Moyer, Haywood, and Pettibone remained in jail, bail having been denied. Messages from socialists all over the world poured in on them. From Maxim Gorky came the telegram: "Greetings to you, my brother Socialists. Courage! The day of justice and deliverance for the oppressed of all the world is at hand."

Jack London's contribution to this struggle had already been made in the form of contributions to the defense fund. Now came his brilliant article, "Something Rotten in Idaho," which appeared in the *Chicago Daily Socialist* on November 4, 1906 while the Supreme Court was at last considering the appeal. It presented a clear-cut indictment of the capitalist system, of capitalist justice and the profit motive. It is a considered, thoughtful, exciting and challenging article, and compels the reader, no matter what his political convictions might be, to draw the conclusion that three workers were in danger of dying for a crime they had never committed because they stood "between the mine owners and a pot of money." It ranks as one of the finest pieces of working-class propaganda London ever turned out and stands as a testimonial to his devotion to the labor movement and his readiness to use his great talent in its behalf. It was a major contribution in the struggle which eventually resulted in the freeing of the three men.

On December 3, 1906, the Supreme Court denied the appeal by a vote of eight to one. A few months later, in February, 1907, London spoke at a mass meeting, held under the auspices of the Socialist Party, to commemorate the first anniversary of the kidnapping and to push on the movement to free the victims. ". . . If the work of freeing Moyer and Haywood and Pettibone is to be carried to a successful conclusion," he cried, "we must lift up not only our fingers but our fists!" He qualified the statement the next day in an interview with a reporter from the *San Francisco Examiner*, but if anyone thought that this signified that Jack London had lost his belief in militant socialism, the appearance of *The Iron Heel,* the most revolutionary novel in American literature, was swiftly to change his mind.

February of 1908 saw the book published which brought lasting fame to London's name the world over, *The Iron Heel,* a rare and prophetic novel. It was written during the summer of 1906 but it was the product of several years of thought and study. With an amazing insight into the mechanism of the capitalist system, London was able to catch tendencies in motion in modern society which went unnoticed by most of his socialist colleagues.

In his first important socialist essay, "The Question of the Maximum," London warned that the ruling class, faced by an economic crisis and the growing influence of socialism, might quickly place "a strong curb . . . upon the masses till the crisis were past." "It has been done before," he argued. "There is no reason why it should not be done again. . . . In 1871 the soldiers of the economic rulers stamped out, root and branch, a whole generation of militant socialists."

In 1903 London read W. J. Ghent's *Our Benevolent Feudalism* which, though written by a socialist sympathizer, ridiculed the contention of many socialists that the socialist society was about to be realized. It predicted instead a new feudalism dominated by the capitalists in which "labor will be bound to the machine in fashion similar to that in which the earlier serf was bound to the soil." In a review of Ghent's book for the *International Socialist Review,* London had urged his comrades to read and study its thesis with the hope that it would jar some of them out of the delusion that the capitalists were powerless to halt the advance of socialism.

Yet in his enthusiasm over the growth of the socialist movement, London forgot Ghent's prediction. In his explanation of the great socialist vote in 1904, written for the *San Francisco Examiner,* he declared that when the Socialist Party won control of the political machinery of the country at the ballot box, it would proceed "to confiscate, with or without remuneration, all the possessions of the capitalist class which are used in the production and distribution of the necessaries and luxuries of life." How the capitalists would meet this London did not pretend to know, but he was confident that they could not halt the advance of socialism in the United States for the simple reason that this was a new type of revolt, "a democratic revolt" which had to be "fought out with ballots," a "peaceable and orderly revolt at the ballot box, under democratic conditions, where the majority rules." Since the capitalists were in the minority, it would be only a matter of time before the majority of the votes were cast for the Socialist Party after which a new society, "run in the interest of the working class," would be instituted.

London's faith in the triumph of "the democratic revolt" remained unabated throughout most of 1905. Few members of the capitalist class in the United States, he declared in his lectures, were aware of the rising tide of revolution in the political world and those capitalists who saw the threat to their power still believed that they could hold it back by "bribery in every legislature for the purchase of capitalist legislation, bayonets, machine-guns, policemen's clubs, professional strike-breakers, and armed Pinkertons . . ." But such efforts were futile since they only succeeded in turning more and more workers into revolutionists. "The revolution is here, now," London declared confidently. "Stop it who can!"

Yet the more London read and studied contemporary events, the more he began to doubt a peaceful transition into socialism. The brutal suppression of the Russian Revolution of 1905 convinced him that the socialists had to face a fierce and violent struggle by the capitalists to maintain their power. True, the United States was not Russia, for here the workers had the right to vote and could pile up majorities for the Socialist Party in elections. But what if the capitalists should deprive the people of their democratic rights and crush the revolutionary movement by force of arms?

To his dismay, London found during his tour for the Intercollegiate Socialist Society that most of the socialist leaders had not the slightest doubt that, faced by a workers' majority at the polls, the overawed capitalists would permit the socialists to take the control of the means of production out of their hands. They were convinced that capitalism in the United States soon would be peacefully voted out of existence. Was not the Socialist Party making headway at the polls? Were not mayors, aldermen, councilmen, and a few members of state legislatures being elected on the socialist ticket? Next came Congress, and as soon as the national legislature was dominated by the socialists, socialism would be on the way in. "When we get Congress," London heard these socialists say, "we can get socialism."

London quickly saw through these delusions. He determined to show these reformist socialists who naïvely believed that the revolution could be brought simply by electing enough socialist congressmen, that the capitalists would not sit by and calmly watch their control of society eliminated by legislative enactments. The capitalist class then would resort to violence to prevent the "democratic revolt" from moving forward, would strike back with unprecedented terror and fulfill W. J. Ghent's prediction of a new feudalism. Instead of Ghent's "Benevolent Feudalism," however, there would emerge the most brutal dictatorship in the history of mankind.

Into *The Iron Heel* London poured his indictment of the socialist leaders for their failure accurately to assay the strength of the capitalists and to prepare to prevent them from abolishing democracy when threatened by the victory of "the democratic revolt." Into this novel he also put his belief in the eventual triumph of socialism, for nothing that had happened in the world had lessened London's confidence that in the end the working class would triumph.

The Iron Heel is the name that London gives to the oligarchy of American capitalists who seized power when there was danger of a socialist victory at the polls. He describes the crushing of labor by this oligarchy during the years between 1912 and 1932 and the terrible and bitter conflict between the socialist underground and the forces of dictatorship. In 1932, when the book ends abruptly, the Oligarchy has undermined the first revolt of the socialist revolutionaries; but secretly they plan the second revolt.

The novel purports to be derived from a manuscript discovered in "the fourth century of the era of Brotherhood which dates the final triumph of socialist democracy" when the promise of socialism is being realized. It is written by Avis, the "gently nurtured wife" of the leader of the second revolt, Ernest Everhard. Throughout the work are footnotes which are intended to interpret various obsolete references for readers who live under socialism. The comments, drawn from his extensive file of newspaper clippings and government documents, are devastating notes on conditions in Jack London's times and are set forth with so keen a satiric sense as to give them place among the most brilliant indictments of capitalism ever written. Through this medium London presented his ablest application of Marxist theory to American conditions.

He introduces his hero, Ernest Everhard as "a superman, a blond beast such as Nietzsche described, and in addition he was aflame with democracy." According to Ernest Untermann, who spent several years with London on his ranch after 1910, Everhard was a composite of three people: Jack London, Eugene V. Debs, and Untermann him-self. Whomever London patterned his hero after he is not very im-portant, for his characterization of him is a political one. We come to know him through his political acts, his courage, his loyalty, his comradeship and his devotion to the struggle for socialism and free-dom. He starts as a wooden image rather than a real character, but as the story unfolds he grows in reality until at the end we begin to get close to him in a personal and intimate way.

Everhard is introduced to the reader at a dinner at the home of John Cunningham, a distinguished physicist and professor at the University of California at Berkeley. There he first meets his future wife, Avis Cunningham, his host's daughter. A discussion develops among some ministers present about the working class and its rela-tion to the church. Everhard is quiet, listening. Finally he bursts out with a scathing attack on the assembled churchmen, telling them that they do not know what they are talking about, that they are merely metaphysicians, each snug in a private world, and knowing nothing of the real world about them. He goes further and charges that the church preaches in the interest of the upper class, the class that supports it. "You belong in the enemy's camp," he tells them bluntly. "You have nothing in common with the working class. . . . Be true to your salt and your hire; guard with your preaching, the interests of your employers, but do not come down to the working class and serve as false leaders. . . ."

Later in a separate discussion with Bishop Morehouse, Everhard asserts that the church no longer teaches Christ, and that the work-ingmen do not wish to have anything to do with an institution which "condones the frightful brutality and savagery with which the capi-talist class treats the working class." He challenges the Bishop to protest against the exploitation of labor, against children toiling in the Southern cotton mills, and against other evils in society, assuring him that it would cost him his post. The Bishop accepts the challenge, determined to prove that the church was not silent in the midst of human suffering. Everhard also challenges Avis Cunningham to learn the full story of a worker in the Sierra Mills, in which the Cunning-hams have investments, who lost his arm and was turned out without a penny. Avis, too, accepts the challenge.

Avis' awakening to the realities of life occurs first. She visits Jack-son, the worker who had lost his arm, discovers that accidents in the Mills were quite common and that the maiming of hundreds of workers, including children, could be traced to the negligence of the company. She also discovers that the evidence presented at the trial to prevent Jackson from collecting damages was all fixed, and she hears Colonel Ingram, the company lawyer, coolly admit that the injured worker should have received damages. Then when Avis writes "a quiet, restrained, dispassionate account" of Jackson's case in which she simply sets forth the facts, she discovers that no newspaper will publish her communication, and learns from a reporter friend that all the papers are "solid with the corporations," and that any editor who printed her material would lose his job.

Thus Avis begins "to see through the appearance of the society" in which she has lived. And the reader gets a simple but dramatic lesson on factory conditions and on the control of the courts and the press by the corporations. Later, along with Bishop Morehouse, the reader learns of the control of the church by the same forces. When the Bishop, having been shown the conditions of the working class in his community, attempts to apply his Christianity literally—to feed the poor, welcome the sinful and humble, and champion the cause of the downtrodden, he is put in a madhouse.

Ernest Everhard is invited to speak before "The Philomaths," an organization of the wealthiest business men of the community with "a sprinkling of scholars to give it intellectual tone." He starts, hesitant, to disarm his listeners into believing him a shy, innocent and ignorant dreamer. He tells them of his life as a worker, and his struggle to secure an education, of his contacts with the upper class and of his consequent disillusionment. From novels he had read he had thought them all fine, noble and intelligent. Instead he found them to be crooked, rotten, selfish and stupid. He had seen ministers of the Gospel dismissed because they refused to heed the biddings of the wealthy, and professors "broken on the wheel of university subservience to the ruling class." In disgust he joined the socialist movement, and a new world opened before his eyes.

His audience remains unmoved; neither his denunciation of the greed and stupidity of the upper class nor his exposition of the spirit of the working class has touched them. Then Ernest tells them about the revolution; he indicts the entire capitalist class, charging it with mismanagement for compelling people to live in poverty when the productive forces of society can provide all with a decent standard of living. He tells them, too, of the determination of the working class to take over the management of society from the capitalist class, and he ends, as did London so often in his own lectures, with the words: "This is the revolution, my masters. Stop it if you can."

The audience is instantly in an uproar. One after another they seek to demolish Everhard's arguments, but he answers them with pitiless logic and they resort to personal invective. Then one of the capitalists who has remained cool throughout the heated exchange rises and says:

> *This, then, is our answer. We have no words to waste on you. When you reach out your vaunted strong hands for our palaces and purpled ease, we will show you what strength is. In roar of shell and shrapnel and in whine of machine-guns will your answer be couched. We will grind you revolutionists down under our heel, and we shall walk upon your faces. The world is ours, we are its lords, and ours it shall remain. . . .*

Everhard replies that the working class will triumph through the power of the ballot. "What if you do get a majority, a sweeping majority, on election day," comes the immediate response. "Suppose we refuse to turn the government over to you after you have captured it at the ballot-box." Then, retorts Everhard, the answer of the working class on that day will come "in roar of shrapnel and in whine of machine-guns. . . ."

At another meeting, this time of small business men and farmers, Everhard calls the middle class "The Machine-Breakers." They know that their existence as a class is rapidly coming to an end, and in their desperate desire for survival are bent on turning back the wheels of progress by breaking up the trusts. He tells them that they are tilting against windmills, that they cannot turn back the tides of economic evolution which made inevitable the rise of the trusts and sounded the doom of the small capitalists. To their cry, "What are we to do then?" he advises them to join the socialists, take over the ownership of the trusts and utilize their abilities for the benefit of all the people rather than for a handful of capitalists. Then he gives them a lesson in Marxism, presenting arguments to prove that capitalism will inevitably break down under its own contradictions and will give way to socialism. He bases this on a mathematical formulation of the Marxist theory of surplus value. Since capitalists do not pay their workers enough to permit them to buy back all that they produce, a large surplus of manufactured goods is piled up each year. The surplus must be exported. Yet soon every nation under capitalism will be in the same predicament, each having its own surplus to export. What then, he asks; and answers that in order to keep prices up and profits secure, it will be necessary to throw the surplus in the sea: "Throw every year hundreds of millions of dollars' worth of shoes and wheat and clothing and all the commodities of commerce into the sea."

Finally, Everhard warns his middle class audience that if they do not soon unite with the workers to achieve socialism, the entire population "will be crushed under the iron heel of a despotism as relentless and terrible as any despotism that has blackened the pages of the history of man."

It does not take long for Everhard's warning to be realized. The Oligarchy starts to crack down, using the entire force of the state to repress rebels and to still all voices which threaten its wealth and power. Social ostracism is the first weapon; then loss of jobs, finally bare-faced and brutal persecution. Vigilante groups, waving American flags and singing patriotic songs, destroy the socialist presses and break up the meetings of labor and radical groups. Strikes are viciously smashed by the police, the militia and the army; workers are wounded and killed and thousands of strikers are herded into concentration camps. The mass of the population is gradually enslaved, but no protests are uttered by the moulders of public opinion, the press, the church and the educators. Anyone who dares to lift his voice in behalf of freedom is deprived of his livelihood or imprisoned.

And while all this transpires the progressive groups are scarcely aware of the powerful forces they are combating and, because of the step-by-step character of the repression, are unable to foresee the ultimate goal of the Oligarchy—the compete overthrow of all democratic processes and the institution of a dictatorship. The socialists and the trade unionists still pin their faith on the ballot box as the solution. But Everhard warns them that the Iron Heel will trample the people's right to vote and that they must be prepared for revolutionary action to prevent it. "In this," writes London, "he was in advance of his party. His fellow-socialists could not agree with him. They still insisted that victory could be gained through the elections. . . . Ernest could not get them seriously to fear the coming of the Oligarchy. They were stirred by him, but they were too sure of their own strength. There was no room in their theoretical social evolution for an oligarchy, therefore the Oligarchy could not be." They would send him to Congress and all would be well.

Then the Plutocracy of America clashes with the German Plutocracy in competition for the same markets. The press and other agencies whip up the war spirit since the ruling class hopes to divert the workers from their enemy at home to its enemy abroad. But the workers of both countries are not so easily fooled. They call a general strike, and the war is stopped before a shot is fired. But the Oligarchy still has a hidden weapon. It buys out the key unions by granting them concessions in the form of higher wages, shorter hours and better working conditions. The solidarity of labor is thereby broken, and the weaker unions crushed.

And still the socialists and the trade union leaders cling to their faith in the ballot. Only Everhard shakes his head. "How many rifles have you got? Do you know where you can get plenty of lead?" he asks when the socialists tell him they will triumph at the polls.

Events draw swiftly to a head. Fifty socialist congressmen are elected. But they are powerless, being in the minority. Slowly the work of destruction proceeds. The labor movement, split and weakened, is crushed; its leaders are arrested, jailed and secretly executed. Finally, labor wakes up and makes a stand. But it is hopeless, for it has come too late. The Iron Heel wreaks on the workers the most awful vengeance. The Mercenaries, a professional soldiery, mow down the revolutionists. In Chicago where a Commune is formed the bloody warfare reaches its height. The city is left a shambles. Labor fights to the last ditch, but to no avail. The socialists, led by Everhard, resort to individual terrorism in their effort to fight back.

> *And through it all moved the Iron Heel, impassive and deliberate, shaking up the whole fabric of the social structure in its search for the comrades, combing out the Mercenaries, the labor castes, and all its secret services, punishing without mercy and without malice, suffering in silence all retaliations that were made upon it, and filling the gaps in its fighting line as fast as they appeared.*

The book ends on this first defeat of the working class. This was followed by a second revolt, as crushingly defeated as was the first, but the events of the book deal only with the first revolt. Everhard was executed by the Oligarchy sometime during the year 1932, while making plans for the second revolt. He dies convinced that in the end the Iron Heel will be crushed: "We have lost a battle, we shall win the war. Lost for this time, but not forever! We have learned many things. Tomorrow the cause will rise once more, stronger in wisdom, and in discipline."

The closing sections of the novel in which London pictures the conditions of the masses after they are reduced to slavery, and portrays the work of the underground, are among the finest pieces of imaginative writing in all literature. The description of imaginary civil war in Chicago is masterly. It is unfortunate, however, that this section of the novel is weakened by London's treatment of the People of the Abyss as a "Roaring Abysmal Beast" moving about with only the aim of destruction in mind and powerless to serve any purpose other than that of providing cannon-fodder for the Mercenaries.

London spent several months writing *The Iron Heel,* fully aware that no publisher might accept it, that no magazine would dare to serialize it, that it would intensify the attacks upon him in the bourgeois press and seriously impair the sale of his other works. Yet he had to get this one book out of his system as his contribution to the success of the social revolution and his warning to the socialist movement that reformism would lead to world-wide disaster for the working class. Fortunately, Macmillan agreed to publish it. Brett's only request was that London delete a footnote which might land both author and publisher in jail. Jack's reply was characteristic: "If they find me guilty of contempt I'd be only too glad to do six months in jail, during which time I could write a couple of books and do no end of reading."

The book met with instant derision by the majority of the critics. The *Indianapolis News* was one of the few papers to praise it. "Power is certainly the keynote of this book," it said. "Every word tingles with it; it is so strong that it is almost brutal. But it is a great book, one that deserves to be read and pondered. . . . The lift of the book sweeps the reader to his feet; it contains a mighty lesson and a most impressive warning." Elsewhere the book was denounced as reckless sensationalism, dishonest, a dull tract masquerading as a novel. *The Dial* declared that "such books as this . . . have a mischievous influence upon unbalanced minds, and we cannot but deplore their multiplication." *The Independent* concluded that "semi-barbarians, to whom this sort of stuff appeals, may possibly tear down our civilization; they will never lay a single brick of a nobler civilization." *The Outlook* summed up the viewpoint of the press with the observation:

". . . as a work of fiction it has little to commend it, and as a socialist
tract it is distinctly unconvincing."

The socialists were divided in their reactions. The more militant
leaders like Eugene Debs, Bill Haywood and Mary Marcy praised it
unstintingly and urged that its lessons be taken to heart by the entire
movement. But the middle class leaders of the Party were even more
vehement in their denunciations than the bourgeois critics. Here the
Socialist Party was making headway at the polls and along came
Jack London and took the edge off these victories with the pessimism
and black despair of *The Iron Heel*. What would happen to those
who had joined the movement because they were led to believe that
in this country socialism was a matter of a few years of peaceful
transition from capitalism and who were convinced that though the
capitalists would resist, the will of the voters at the ballot box would
prevail? Writing in the *International Socialist Review*, John Spargo
admitted that there was literary skill in "this ingenious and stirring
romance," but disagreed violently with those socialists who hailed it
as a "great addition to the literature of Socalist propaganda." "The
picture he gives," Spargo went on, "is well calculated, it seems to me,
to repel many whose addition to our forces is sorely needed; it gives
a new impetus to the old and generally discarded cataclysmic theory;
it tends to weaken the political Socialist movement by discrediting the
ballot and to encourage the chimerical and reactionary notion of
physical force, so alluring to a certain type of mind . . ."

London emphatically denied that his message in *The Iron Heel*
signified an abandonment on his part of a belief in political action.
"I believe there is much to be gained by entering political cam-
paigns," he told a socialist reporter several years later. "The real
advantage, in my opinion, is the great opportunity to educate the
workers to an understanding of the wrong of the present system and
the meaning of class consciousness." In the same interview he repeated
the basic message of *The Iron Heel*:

> *History shows that no master class is ever willing to let go
> without a quarrel. The capitalists own the governments, the
> armies and the militia. Don't you think the capitalists will use
> these institutions to keep themselves in power? I do.*

It was the capitalist class not the workers, London insisted, who
would use violence; in their attempt to prevent the democratic will
of the people from being exercised they would institute a reign of ter-

ror to destroy the movements that threatened their power. The years have proved Jack London's picture in *The Iron Heel* to be tragically correct. We have but to substitute the word "fascism" for "oligarchy" and *The Iron Heel* becomes a living picture of what actually happened in the past two decades. It is true that London did not foresee the brutal forms which fascism would take in our time. Yet, despite many differences between what happened in Germany, Italy and Spain and what is pictured in this book, it is probably the most amazingly prophetic work of the twentieth century. Since the advent of fascism, radicals the world over have come to realize the validity of Jack London's prophecies. In 1924, after fascism had come to Italy, Anatole France wrote in an introduction to a new edition of *The Iron Heel*: "Alas, Jack London had that particular genius which perceived what is hidden from the common herd, and possessed a special knowledge enabling him to anticipate the future. He foresaw the assemblage of events which is but now unrolling to our view."

Jack London was not in the country when *The Iron Heel* appeared. On April 23, 1907 he hoisted Jimmy Hopper's football sweater for a pennant and sailed for Hawaii and the South Seas on what was to be a seven year voyage around the world. The *Socialist Voice* of Oakland bade him a mixed farewell:

> *Goodby, Jack, Goodby! The* Snark, *flying the red flag, weighed anchor April 22, and Jack London and his wife are now at sea. Roosevelt will be glad to know there is one less "undesirable citizen" in the country. To us Comrade London's departure is a source both of congratulation and regret. London goes into a field of wider usefulness to the cause of socialism, and we are glad. Our only regret is that we shall miss his cheering personal contact.* Socialist Voice *has had many occasions to be grateful to Comrade London for substantial aid, as well as for encouragement. We hope the old world will wag right for you, Jack, and send you back to us the same big-hearted, clear-headed, hard-fisted fellow you now are. Good Luck!*

Amidst incredible chaos and danger, with his boat threatening any moment to sink under him, and his crew sea-sick, London sat down and began work on *Martin Eden*. The twenty-eight days before Hawaii was reached was one long nightmare. But there was the consolation that now at last in Hawaii he could do his daily stint on the novel, turn out articles about the voyage for the magazines and newspapers and write short stories without worrying about leaks, nonfunctioning bathrooms, spoiled food and filthy quarters. Moreover, the warm welcome extended to London and his crew by the "sweet people" of the "sweet land" made him forget the terrible voyage. One week was spent gathering material for an article on the leper island, Molokai, written at the request of the lepers with whom Jack and Charmian mingled freely. This article, "The Lepers of Molokai," in which he paid tribute to these outcasts who managed to create a happy community on the island, is one of the most sensitive pieces of writing to come out of the cruise.

But while Jack was adventuring in Hawaii, the Marquesas and Tahiti, his estate at home was being run into the ground by his sponging fair-weather friends and relatives. So much of his money was being squandered that in the first week of 1908, while in Tahiti, he learned that all he had in the world was sixty-six dollars. Yet a month before he had received almost six thousand dollars in royalties.

Jack decided to return to San Francisco to straighten out his affairs. He set sail from Tahiti on the *S.S. Mariposa,* landed in San Francisco, immediately wired Brett at Macmillan for an advance against the almost completed *Martin Eden,* paid off the most pressing of his debts, put his affairs into a semblance of order, and within ten days was back on the *Mariposa* for Tahiti to pick up the threads of his projected seven-year voyage around the world. He left behind him scores of enraged socialists who castigated him for deserting the movement.

There are many contradictions in the life of Jack London, but it is difficult to find one that equals his conduct in the South Seas. Everywhere he went, Fiji, the Marquesas, Samoa, and Hawaii, wherever he could gather a group of white men together, he would lecture them on Revolution and expound the class struggle and the battle for socialism. Yet he took part in the "blackbirding" expeditions which recruited natives as slave laborers for the copra * plantations. And in none of the articles or stories which came out of the cruise of the *Snark* is there any criticism of the effects of the white man's "civilization" upon the natives.

On one score London was consistent: come what might, through periods of skin ulcers and yaws, he continued his daily output of a

* Copra. The dried coconut palm kernel used in soap making.

thousand words. But against malaria even he was helpless, and for months he was as often on his back as on his feet. By September, 1908 he was in constant pain, the victim of a strange disease which no one could diagnose. Finally, too ill to seek further adventure, he arranged with a retired sea captain to watch over the *Snark*, and engaged passage for himself, Charmian, Martin Johnson and his servant, Makata, for Sydney, Australia.

London spent five weeks in a Sydney hospital, but to no avail; his affliction baffled Australian specialists. He remained in Sydney five more months, too sick to do much writing or reading. Yet it is amazing that in spite of a malady which caused his hands to swell to twice their natural size and his skin to peel off in layers, he turned out a penetrating article for the Sydney *Star* contrasting strike methods in the United States and Australia. No one reading the article could possibly guess that the author was a sick and discouraged young man. It has the old London vitality; the vigorous assertion of the class struggle; the indictment of capitalism for mismanagement, and the prediction that "the future belongs to labor." London answers the question, "Will industrial peace ever come?" with the observation:

> *And the only answer is that it will never come so long as the present system of industrial production obtains. Human nature will not change. Capital will continue to want all it can get, and labor will continue to want all it can get. And on both sides they will fight for it. No, the lion and the lamb will never lie down together in vegetarian pastures.*
>
> *"Then must we forever endure the irrational anarchy of strikes and lockouts?" some one asks. Not so, is the answer. There are two ways by which industrial peace may be achieved. Either capital will own labor absolutely, and there will be no more strikes, or labor will own capital absolutely, and there will be no more strikes. . . ."*

In contrast with his treatment of this theme in *The Iron Heel*, it is interesting to note that London was now convinced that it was "illogical to think of capital absolutely owning labor," for this "would mean chattel slavery, a trend backward to primeval night out of which civilisation has emerged." Evidently while he could predict fascism in his novel, London really could not conceive that mankind would permit these horrors to come to pass. He was spared the revelation that that which he termed "illogical" would become a reality.

London decided to get home to California and sent Martin Johnson to the Solomon Islands to bring the *Snark* back to Sydney. There she was sold at auction for $3,000 and put into service as a blackbirder among the Solomon Islands. This was the end of a ship built by a man who just a few weeks before had written in the Sydney *Star:* "It would seem from reading the past, that the future belongs to labor." On July 23, 1909, two and a quarter years after he had set sail with such enthusiasm for a voyage around the world, Jack London landed in San Francisco, discouraged, his health shot to pieces, deeply in debt, and the magazines and newspapers convinced that his best writing was behind him.

During his twenty-five months' experience in the South Seas, London wrote three books which can be regarded as direct products of the voyage: the articles that made up *The Cruise of the Snark,* the stories in *South Sea Tales* and the novel *Adventure.* With the exception of "The Lepers of Molokai" in *The Cruise of the Snark* and four of the stories in *South Sea Tales,* these books added little to London's literary stature. And so much of this writing is saturated with his chauvinistic conceit of the supremacy of the Anglo-Saxon race that these books also added little to his stature as a socialist. In only four stories —"The House of Mapuhi," "Mauki," "Samuel," and "The Seed of McCoy"—is the native population portrayed sympathetically. In all the rest, the native is servile and the white man the master.

Martin Eden, as we have seen, was started and completed during the voyage, but it is based entirely on London's earlier life and is in no sense a product of the expedition. Yet long after all of the articles and most of the stories which came directly from the voyage would be forgotten, *Martin Eden* would still be counted among the great American novels.

It is, of course, the most autobiographical of Jack London's novels, dealing with the self-education of a sailor and recounting in the process most of London's own struggles to become a writer. The title character, a poorly-educated sailor, saves the life of Arthur Morse, a well-to-do young man. He is introduced into Morse's home, a place of wealth and culture, where he meets Mrs. Morse, a typical "good wife and mother" of the upper middle class, Mr. Morse, a well-intentioned but unimaginative business man, Arthur's brothers, pleasant young college-boys with no vitality in them, and Ruth, the "pale, ethereal creature with wide spiritual blue eyes and a wealth of golden hair" whom he likens "to a pale gold flower upon a slender stem" and promptly worships. Awkward and embarrassed, ungrammatical and crude though he is, there is about him such virility and an air of romance arising from harsh adventures in far places of the world, that Ruth, to her horror, feels the strong attraction of his physical being. Martin's love for her and his admiration for her gracious way of life, stimulate him to educate himself and become a cultured individual able to move about with ease in her home. Ruth tutors and advises him at first, but is soon outstripped by a more intense intellect which, thwarted for twenty years, seizes upon culture with all its pent-up force. With an incredible hunger, Martin devours Spencer, Darwin, Huxley, Marx, Hegel and a huge and varied body of sociological, philosophical and literary works.

It is not long before Martin Eden begins to see through the bourgeois hypocrisy of the Morse family and to realize that Ruth, his idol, shares their narrowness and smugness. But his love for her becomes more understanding as he recognizes her intellectual and human inadaquacies. Their engagement is a blow to the father and mother, but they decide to say nothing, biding their time in the belief that the uncouth Eden will dispose of himself.

Burning to become a writer, Martin Eden devotes over a year of gruelling labor and incredible self-denial to his chosen task—living in a hovel on the meagre meals he cooks himself, sleeping five hours a night and besieging the editors with manuscripts. But he receives neither encouragement nor understanding and sympathy from Ruth. On various occasions he reads her some of his stories whose quality she is totally unable to judge. She recognizes the power of the writing, but not the beauty in its realism; indeed, his attempts at beauty in realism provoke her indignant comments "degrading" and "nasty."

The break between the two comes with Martin's persistent refusal, in the face of constant rejections by the editors, to surrender his literary ambition and take a job. Just on the verge of his becoming a successful writer, Ruth breaks the engagement.

Brissenden, the consumptive poet and cynic, alone recognizes Martin Eden's gifts, and he seeks to persuade him to join the socialist movement, predicting disillusionment for Martin if he does succeed as a writer and has nothing to hold him to life. But Martin Eden refuses to heed his advice. "As for myself," he says ,"I am an individualist. I believe the race is to the swift, the battle to the strong. Such is the lesson I have learned from biology, or at least I think I have learned. As I said, I am an individualist, and individualism is the hereditary and eternal foe of socialism."

Brissenden dies before his prophecy is fulfilled. A controversial essay which has a phenomenal sale brings Martin's name to the attention of the editors, and he is overwhelmed with requests for material. Martin throws back at the editors the dozens of manuscripts which have been rejected and this time they are gobbled up. He becomes rich overnight even though he has written nothing new. The desire to beat the enemy at his own game becomes his major concern.

But soon a great weariness overtakes him. He is invited to the wealthiest homes for dinner, but now that he no longer fasts by necessity, it leaves him unmoved. He is indifferent even to Ruth, and refuses to renew their relationship when she comes to see him. Basically his spiritual weariness arises from his resentment that no one except Brissenden (who is dead) has respected him before he was publicly recognized. He hates the thought that he is being recognized not for his ability but because his name is in demand.

> *Invitations to dinner poured in on Martin; and the more they poured, the more he puzzled. He sat, the guest of honor, at an Arden Club banquet, with men of note whom he had heard about and read about all his life; and they told him how, when they had read "The Ring of Bells" in the* Transcontinental, *and "The Peri and the Pearl" in* The Hornet, *they had immediately picked him for a winner. My God! and I was hungry and in rags, he thought to himself. Why didn't you give me a dinner then? Then was the time. It was work performed. If you are feeding me now for work performed, why did you not feed me then when I needed it? Not one word in "The Ring of Bells," nor in "The Peri and the Pearl" has been changed. No; you're not feeding me now for work performed. You are feeding me because everybody else is feeding me and because it is an honor to feed me. You are feeding me now because you are herd animals; because you are part of the mob; because the one blind, automatic thought in the mob-mind just now is to feed me. And where does Martin Eden and the work Martin Eden performed come in in all this? he asked himself plaintively, then arose to respond cleverly and wittily to a clever and witty toast.*

As Brissenden had predicted, Martin Eden's success was more

disillusioning to him than all his previous defeats. He refuses to write another word, winds up his business affairs, and sails for the South Seas. Enroute, however, weariness overcomes him and he slips through a porthole and vanishes into the midnight depths:

> *Down, down, he swam until his arms and legs grew tired and hardly moved. He knew that he was deep. The pressure on his ear-drums was a pain, and there was a buzzing in his head. His endurance was faltering, but he compelled his arms and legs to drive him deeper until his will snapped and the air drove from his lungs in a great explosive rush. The bubbles rubbed and bounded like tiny balloons against his cheeks and eyes as they took their upward flight. Then came pain and strangulation. This hurt was not death, was the thought that oscillated through his reeling consciousness. Death did not hurt. It was life, the pangs of life, this awful, suffocating feeling; it was the last blow life could deal him.*
>
> *His wilful hands and feet began to beat and churn about, spasmodically and feebly. But he had fooled them and the will to live that made them beat and churn. He was too deep down. They could never bring him to the surface. He seemed floating languidly in a sea of dreamy vision. Colors and radiances surrounded him and bathed him and pervaded him. What was that? It seemed a lighthouse; but it was inside his brain—a flashing, bright white light. It flashed swifter and swifter. There was a long rumble of sound, and it seemed to him that he was falling down a vast and interminable stairway. And somewhere at the bottom he fell into darkness. That much he knew. He had fallen into darkness. And at the instant he knew, he ceased to know.*

The reaction of the critics bewildered and angered Jack London. It was not so much that hardly any reviewer had a good word to say for the book or that they sneered at the plot and declared that he was "quite at sea" when he tried "to write about that ordinary society which is variously described as decent, as respectable, as cultured, or as good, and, in his language, as bourgeois." This he had come to expect. What aroused his anger was that most of the critics, including Socialist reviewers, attacked the novel as an apology for individualism and as proof that London had abandoned his belief in socialism. Again and again London was to assert that *Martin Eden* was the most misunderstood of all his books. In the flyleaf of one copy of the book he wrote on April 4, 1910: "This is a book that missed fire with a majority of the critics. Written as an indictment of individualism, it was accepted as an indictment of socialism; written to show that man cannot live for himself alone, it was accepted as a demonstration that individualism made for death. Had Martin Eden been a socialist he would not have died." A few years later in *John Barleycorn* he pointed out that when pessimism overwhelmed him and he was about to seek Martin Eden's way out, one thing had saved him—the People!

> *I meditated suicide coolly, as a Greek philosopher might. My regret was that there were too many dependent directly upon me for food and shelter for me to quit living. But that was sheer morality. What really saved me was the one remaining illusion—THE PEOPLE.*
>
> *The things that I had fought for and burned my midnight oil for, had failed me. Success—I despised it. Recognition—it was dead ashes. Society, men and women above the ruck and muck of the water-front and the forecastle. I was appalled by their unlovely mental mediocrity. Love of woman—it was like the rest. Money—I could sleep in only one bed at a time, and of what worth was an income of a hundred porter-houses a day when I could eat only one? Art, culture—in the face of the iron facts of biology such things were ridiculous, the exponents of such things only the more ridiculous.*
>
> *From the foregoing it can be seen how very sick I was. I was born a fighter. The things I had fought for had proved not worth the fight. Remained the PEOPLE. My fight was finished, yet something was left still to fight for—the PEOPLE.*
>
> *But the PEOPLE saved me. By the PEOPLE I was hand-cuffed to life. There was still one fight left in me, and there was the thing for which to fight. I threw all precaution to the winds, threw myself with fiercer zeal in the fight for socialism. . . .*

The critics, however, can hardly be blamed for missing London's message in *Martin Eden;* indeed, it is likely that the average reader today still comes away from the book without the slightest conception that it was meant to be an attack on individualism. Actually, if it was London's aim to make converts for socialism in *Martin Eden* he chose peculiar ways of doing it. It is true that in the description of the discussion at the rooms of Kreis, a professor fired from the university for his radical views, there is a brilliant contrast between the superficial conversation at the Morse's and the keen witty remarks of the "rebels of one variety or another." But of the entire group only Brissenden is a socialist. And London's picture of Brissenden, the one socialist with whom Martin Eden has any real contact, is scarcely one to arouse enthusiasm for the movement. Brissenden explains that he is a socialist "because socialism is inevitable; because the present rotten and irrational system cannot endure; because the day is past for your man on horseback." But he has only contempt for the people, refers to them as "slaves," and freely admits: "Of course I don't like the crowd, but what's a poor chap to do?" Nothing in Brissenden reminds one of Ernest Everhard in *The Iron Heel* who is drawn to socialism by his love for the people and a determination to share in their struggles.

The only other socialist described in some detail in *Martin Eden* is a speaker at an open meeting of the Oakland local of whom London writes: "The speaker, a clever Jew, won Martin's admiration at the same time that he aroused his antagonism. The man's stooped and narrow shoulders and weazened chest proclaimed him the true child of the crowded ghetto, and strong on Martin was the age-long struggle of the feeble, wretched slaves against the lordly handful of men who had ruled over them and would rule over them to the end of time. To Martin this withered wisp of a creature was a symbol. He was the figure that stood forth representative of the whole miserable mass of weaklings and inefficients who perished according to biological law on the ragged confines of life. They were the unfit. . . ." But London does not tell us that the speaker is a "symbol" of the exploitation of labor under capitalism, nor does he even reveal what there was about him that won Martin's admiration. It is hardly surprising then that so many readers have left the account of the meeting of the Oakland local with the feeling that socialists were indeed "queer" people. How the reader can then possibly conclude that the tragedy of Martin Eden's life lay in his refusal to associate himself with such people is something which Jack London never bothered to explain.

Thus while *Martin Eden* is today regarded by many critics to be Jack London's most mature work and while it does contain a brilliant picture of the struggles of a worker to become educated, to make a living by writing, to become a success, it is also in many ways one of

the least successful of his works. For it has been seized upon time
and again to prove exactly the opposite of what the author said he
wished to demonstrate.

Three short stories written soon after *Martin Eden* was completed
were proof that London had not lost his ability to bring his message
home clearly to his readers, and consequently all three, "The Dream
of Debs," "South of the Slot" and "The Strength of the Strong," received much more attention in the socialist movement than the
autobiographical novel.

"The Dream of Debs," published in the *International Socialist
Review* in January-February, 1909, is an extremely readable and exciting story of a nation-wide general strike as seen through the eyes
of the rich in San Francisco. The events take place sometime in the
1940's after the American Federation of Labor has been destroyed
by its class-collaborationist president and its place taken by the
I.L.W., "the biggest and solidest organization of labor the United
States has ever seen." Every detail of the strike has been worked out
in advance; it is conducted in an orderly and peaceful manner and
the workers win by starving the capitalists into submission.

The description of events during the strike reveals that London
had done considerable reading on the tactics of a general strike. Transportation is dead; the rich join the poor on the bread lines; hordes of
city dwellers leave San Francisco and the countryside is devastated
and cleaned out, and finally, after the outburst of violence among
the slum people and the upper classes, the Employers' Association is
forced to come to terms with the I.L.W. and the strike is over. The
rich narrator's closing sentence, is typical of the reaction of employers at all stages in the history of the labor movement: "The
tyranny of organized labor is getting beyond human endurance.
Something must be done."

In a review of Leroy Scott's *The Walking Delegate* in the *San
Francisco Examiner* of May 28, 1905, London had sharply criticized
leaders of the American Federation of Labor "whose corrupt dealings
throw much of odium upon the trade union movement," and had
stressed that such leaders shared no small part of the responsibility
for the exploitation of labor. Now in "The Dream of Debs" he
demonstrated how a militant labor movement, led by honest men,
could gain important victories for the working class. True, he ex-
aggerated the supineness of the government in the face of the general
strike and his love of the romantic led him to show the workers

carrying out their plans with all the secrecy of a small, underground group. But with these exceptions the story is realistically handled and emerges as a remarkable piece of working-class propaganda clothed as fiction. It was reprinted in pamphlet form and received a wide circulation in labor circles, especially among the members of the I.W.W. after whom London had modelled the militant trade union which led the general strike.

"South of the Slot," published in the *Saturday Evening Post* of May 22, 1909, is a tale of the class struggle in San Francisco. The "Slot" is an iron crack along Market Street, separating the town into two residential sections—one for the rich, and one for the poor. Literally it is the class line of society.

Freddie Drummond, sociology professor at the University of California, an academic, slightly anemic, self-satisfied young writer, takes to crossing the Slot to study social conditions. He assumes the disguise of a truck driver and the name "Big" Bill Totts, a husky, boisterous worker, good fellow and good union man.

As Freddie Drummond he becomes engaged to a registerite damsel named Catherine Van Vorst. As Bill Totts he takes part in strike struggles and becomes friendly with Mary Condon, militant head of the Glove Workers' Union No. 974.

The two personalities come into direct conflict one day when Freddie Drummond and Catherine Van Vorst are driving in her automobile to visit a Boys' Club and are caught between striking workers and the police. The scabs driving the meat wagons are halted by a traffic jam created by a sympathetic coal-driver and teamster. As Freddie and Catherine look on, the police appear to be winning. A policeman has reached the top of the barricade, and has seized a worker. Freddie can stand it no longer. It is "Big" Bill Totts who leaps out of the car, onto the barricade and goes in punching for the workers, knocking down the policeman. Against the police "his onslaught was like a whirlwind. A rush of three more policemen gained the top [of the coal wagon stopped during the fight] and locked with Bill Totts in a gigantic clinch, during which his scalp was opened up by a club, and coat, vest, and half his starched shirt was torn from him. But the three policemen were flung wide and far, and Bill Totts, raining down lumps of coal, held the fort"

After the battle Bill Totts swings out of sight with Mary Condon on his arm. Thus the dual roles have been united in the heat of the class struggle, and a new labor leader arises, Bill Totts by name.

It is a magnificent working-class story showing the inevitable conflict between a worker's personality and the passionless, conservative
professor. In addition, it has one of the most exciting descriptions of
a street fight between workers and police ever written.

"The Strength of the Strong," published in *Hampton's Magazine*
in May, 1910, is one of the best of Jack London's propaganda stories
and is among the finest parables in American literature, ranking
with Edward Bellamy's "Parable of the Water Tank." The story is
set in pre-historic times, in an age when men have just begun to
abandon homes in the trees. Long Beard, an elder of the tribe, teaches
the younger men the meaning of unity and cooperation by a tale of
the old days, of his own youth. Once the tribe consisted of individual
families each hostile and afraid of the other, and each fending for
itself. But they learned the value of cooperation when a united tribe,
the Meat-Eaters, attacked and almost destroyed them. They saw that
"each Meat-Eater had the strength of ten for the ten had fought as
one man." So the tribe held council, drew up a system of self-defense
and formulated a code of laws.

But disunity returned. Among the tribe were the few who were
more interested in their own comfort than in the general welfare.
At first there was plenty to eat for all, but the few greedy ones amassed
all the land and forced the others to work for them. The son of the
chief, Dog-Tooth, demanded to be chief when his father died; another, Big-Fat, who could speak with the spirits of the dead set himself
up as the representative of the gods, and still another, Little Belly,
invented a fish-trap which enabled him to corner the market. The surplus was so great that the workers were no longer paid in kind but in
money. "But," Long Beard recalls, "this was the strange thing: as the
days went by we who were left worked harder and harder, and yet did
we get less and less to eat." The more money the exploiting members
of the tribe accumulated, the less there was for the workers, and the
more the workers produced, the less food they had to eat. As the
surplus increased, wages went still lower and the workers could not
afford to buy back the very food they had produced. So while they
went hungry, food was destroyed to keep prices high.

Inevitably the workers became discontented with their lot, and this
discontent flared into rebellion. But some of the workers were given
favored positions as guards and ordered to kill the rebels. The church
condemned the rebels and preached that God had decreed that the
wiser must rule over the rest. And the Bug, who had gained a reputa-

tion as a singer, sang that the Fish-Eaters were God's chosen people and that it was His will that they destroy the Meat-Eaters. Forgetting their hunger and their grumbling, the workers clamored to be led against the Meat-Eaters. They did not heed the words of one of the workers, Split-Nose, who cried that their real enemies were the rulers of the tribe, that they should take away the power and wealth of the rich, and that they should join forces with the Meat-Eaters instead of fighting them. When the Bug sang that Split-Nose was a menace to the tribe, the starving workers joined in stoning him to death.

But in the end, disunited, weakened by starvation and disease, the workers were unable to resist their enemies. The Meat-Eaters came over the divide and destroyed the tribe. Long Beard, who managed to escape, concludes:

> *Some day . . . all the fools will be dead, and then all live men will go forward. The secret of the strength of the strong will be theirs, and they will add their strength together, so that of all the men in the world not one will fight with another. . . . And all men will be brothers, and no man will lie idle in the sun and be fed by his fellows.*

London made effective use of the past to build his indictment of capitalism, and his simplicity of plot and style as well as his story-telling ability made "The Strength of the Strong" an ideal propaganda piece. Soon after its appearance in *Hampton's Magazine,* it was reprinted as a pamphlet by Charles H. Kerr Company of Chicago, the socialist cooperative publishing house, and became one of the classics of socialist literature.

When London returned from Australia he found the newspapers and magazines hostile or disinterested. But it was not long before he was back in favor with the reading public and being sought after by editors. The California climate helped him to recuperate and when he discovered that the mysterious disease that had afflicted him was caused by nothing more than the ultra-violet rays of the tropical sun, he recaptured his old vitality. He picked up his routine and again turned out a thousand words a day six days a week.

What flowed from Jack London's pen after his return from the South Seas, with a few exceptions, were no better than pot-boilers. Nor is this surprising, considering the growing demand on his pocket-book. The quality of what he wrote did not, in the main, concern him.

He was interested only in the money it would bring in for the upkeep of his ranch and the support of his relatives and numerous retainers who sucked him dry. "I have no unfinished stories," he said frankly during an interview in 1911. "Invariably I complete every one I start. If it's good, I sign it and send it out. If it isn't good, I sign it and send it out." And he had grown to hate his work:

> *I loathe the stuff when I have done it* [he wrote to Upton Sinclair]. *I do it because I want money and it is an easy way to get it. But if I could have my choice about it I never would put pen to paper—except to write a Socialist essay to tell the bourgeois world how much I despise it.*

But he no longer had a choice. Money as such, he wrote in *John Barleycorn,* meant nothing to him. Yet the continuous financial demands made upon him compelled him to earn money by his writing, regardless of whether or not he had any inspiration. By the summer of 1910 he was buying story plots from Sinclair Lewis, rejecting those which were not suited to his temperament and others because he was "too lazy to dig up the requisite data or atmosphere." To young writers eager to learn the secret of success in the profession, he would reply advising them to take their time and, if necessary, to spend a day on a paragraph. But he himself could no longer follow his own advice. Writing was a means of making money, and the more he wrote the more money poured in. The quality no longer mattered.

Of course, London had become so adept that even at his worst he is eminently readable. And in some of the books he wrote in the last years of his life like *Burning Daylight, John Barleycorn, The Valley of the Moon* and *The Star Rover,* there are sections which show that he could still tell a vivid story in a wholly convincing way. Moreover, the descriptions of high finance in *Burning Daylight,* the picture of the life of the workers and of the flaming labor troubles in Oakland in *The Valley of the Moon,* and the terrible indictment of society for its treatment of criminals in *The Star Rover,* are proof that London had not entirely lost the ability to present an important social message. Unfortunately, the realistic observations in these books are usually obscured by unrealistic plots and preposterous characters, the stories often run to seed after promising beginnings, and the writing too frequently reflects London's backward racial prejudices. The truth is that never again was Jack London to attain the literary heights of *The Sea Wolf* and *Martin Eden* or the class-consciousness of *The Iron Heel*.

The decline in London's writings coincides with the waning of his activity in the socialist movement. He contributed financially to the Party and when he drove down to Santa Rosa once a week for relaxation he would discuss socialism with anyone at the bar and "would say things in the presence of judges, chamber of commerce executives and businessmen about how corrupt the capitalist system was." But other than that he did little for the movement, devoting most of his energies to fantastic ventures that he seemed to need to take his mind off the pot-boilers. He grew eucalyptus trees; he raised horses; he tried to make arid land fertile; he made his ranch a combination agricultural laboratory and model community, a utopian colony where he employed men with a genuine love for the soil and built cottages for his workers and schools for their children. But failure after failure struck at him. The money poured out, as through a sieve, and no results were realized.

On August 18, 1913, the magnificent "Wolf House," on which London had spent over $70,000, was completed. The workmen cleaned up and left. During the night the house burned to the ground. From this blow he never recovered. The outer stone shell of the house, which was all that remained of the magnificent mansion, was a symbol of what was left of Jack London.

Many of London's comrades viewed the tragedy as a judgment from heaven against a socialist for building a castle. They resented his having poured so much money into the house, believing that his extravagance gave the Cause unfavorable publicity and that it was hardly fitting for a socialist to spend so much to satisfy personal whims when the Party was desperately in need of funds. London, who always believed that the possession of wealth did not make him a capitalist, replied that he had built the house with money earned by his own labor.

The justification convinced few people, yet it is true that all his wealth came from his own labor. He had no investments and he exploited no one. Furthermore, his generosity was widely known. When he was building "Wolf House" he gave explicit orders that no man applying for work was to be turned away. Every Wobbly who journeyed westward stopped in for a handout at Jack London's place in the Valley of the Moon, and his ranch was a veritable refuge for all the down-and-outers who passed through California. His financial contributions to the movement and to special labor causes continued.

Still the cry that he was an "apostate Socialist" continued and increased as he moved further and further away from the Party. The finishing touch came with his changing attitude towards the Mexican Revolution.

In February, 1911, Jack London had addressed a letter to the "dear, brave comrades of the Mexican Revolution" who had revolted against the dictatorship of General Porfirio Diaz. The stirring letter, first published in the socialist press, had the characteristic London flair:

> *We socialists, anarchists, hobos, chicken thieves, outlaws and undesirable citizens of the United States are with you heart and soul in your efforts to overthrow slavery and autocracy in Mexico. You will notice we are not respectable in these days of the reign of property. All the names you are being called, we have been called. And when graft and greed get up and begin to call names, honest men, brave men, patriotic men and martyrs can expect nothing else than to be called chicken thieves and outlaws.*
>
> *So be it. But I for one wish that there were more chicken thieves and outlaws of the sort that formed the gallant band that took Mexicali, of the sort that is heroically enduring the prison holes of Diaz, of the sort that is fighting and dying and sacrificing in Mexico today.*
>
> *I subscribe myself a chicken thief and revolutionist,*
>
> *Jack London.*

A few weeks later London again expressed his solidarity with the Mexican revolutionists in a newspaper interview during which he also revealed his opposition to American imperialism in Mexico. "I hope the people of the United States," he declared after American troops had been dispatched to Mexico, "will resent this latest action of the United States government in proposing to overawe the Mexican revolutionists, but I'm afraid they will not. The action of the government is logical. It regards dollars, not democracy, and therefore it will send its troops to protect its dollars. It may be necessary to send troops into Mexico to crush the rebellion. Diaz is afraid all hell may break loose. If the United States government wants to invade Mexico, it can find plenty of legal pretexts, but it would be a burning shame.

It might end the revolution, but it certainly cannot crush the revolutionary spirit in Mexico."

London's sympathy for the Mexican Revolution also found expression in one of the short stories written during this period of his career, "The Mexican," published in the *Saturday Evening Post* on August 12, 1913. It describes the work of the Junta operating in the United States in support of the coming Mexican Revolution and, in particular, of one of the members of the organization, the eighteen-year-old Felipe Rivera, who becomes a prize fighter to raise money for guns for the Revolution. In the course of his masterful description of the fight between Rivera and Danny Ward, the coming lightweight champion, London uses the flash-back technique to show what was behind the revolutionary movement in Mexico. As Rivera sits in his corner awaiting the arrival of Danny Ward and his retinue, his mind goes back to his childhood:

> *He saw the white-walled, water-power factories of Rio Blanco. He saw the six thousand workers, starved and wan, and the little children, seven and eight years of age, who toiled long shifts for ten cents a day. He saw the perambulating corpses, the ghastly death's heads of men who labored in the dye rooms. He remembered that he had heard his father call the dye rooms the "suicide holes," where a year was death. . . .*
>
> *Big, hearty Joaquin Fernandez! A large place he occupied in Rivera's visions. He had not understood at the time, but, looking back, he could understand. He could see him setting type in the little printery, or scribbling endless hasty, nervous lines on the much-cluttered desk. And he could see the strange evenings, when workmen, coming secretly in the dark like men who did ill deeds, met with father and talked long hours where he, the muchado, lay not always asleep in the corner. . . .*
>
> *But more visions burned before the eye of Rivera's memory. The strike, or rather, the lockout, because the workers of Rio Blanco had helped their striking brothers of Puebla. The hunger, the expeditions in the hills for berries, the roots and herbs that all ate and that twisted and pained the stomachs of all of them. And then the nightmare; the waste of ground before the company's store; the thousands of starving workers; General Rosalio Martinez and the soldiers of Porfirio Diaz; and the death-spitting rifles that seemed never to cease spitting,*

*while the workers' wrongs were washed and washed again in
their own blood. And that night! He saw the flatcars, piled
high with the bodies of the slain, consigned to Vera Cruz, food
for the sharks of the bay. Again he crawled over the grisly
heaps, seeking and finding, stripped and mangled, his father
and his mother. His mother he especially remembered—only
her face projecting, her body burdened by the weight of dozens
of bodies. Again the rifles of the soldiers of Porfirio Diaz
cracked, and again he dropped to the ground and slunk away
like some hunted coyote of the hills.*

These visions enable Rivera to stand up under Danny Ward's brutal
punishment and, in the end, to knock out the coming champion. Bat-
tered and bruised though he is, Rivera is happy. The five thousand
dollar purse is his. "The guns were his. The revolution could go on."

Two years later Jack London was to hail American action against
the Mexican Revolution. After a series of revolutions and counter-
revolutions, during which American oil and financial interests ma-
neuvered to move in and control the Mexican economy, an incident
occurred which produced American intervention. An affront to an
American naval officer in Tampico was followed by a demand by the
United States that the American flag be saluted. Huerta, then in
power, refused and, on April 21, 1914, American troops seized Vera
Cruz.

In 1911 Jack London would have seen through the "legal pretexts"
which the United States used to justify its flagrant imperialism, would
have joined with other socialists and the trade unions in opposing the
unwarranted action of the Wilson administration, and would have
hailed the fact that when President Wilson asked Congress for permission to raise the army to war strength for the purpose of sending
an expedition to Mexico, Meyer London, the socialist congressman
from New York, cast the only vote recorded in the negative. But Jack
London was too tired, too deeply involved with his ranch and his
retinue of laborers and servants, and had moved too far away from
the active life of the Party, to be concerned about the revolution any
longer. So, on April 16, 1914, when *Collier's Weekly* wired him an
offer of $1100 a week and expenses to report the "war" he jumped at
the chance. He left the next day for Galveston where he was scheduled
to receive his credentials from Washington and from which port he
was to sail by army transport to Vera Cruz.

At Galveston he was forced to wait for his credentials. General Funston, it appeared, was not anxious to bestow a war correspondent's credentials on a man who two years before was reported to have denounced the military life and to have advised everyone to stay out of the army.

In October, 1913 the *International Socialist Review* had carried an article entitled "The Good Soldier" by Jack London. It urged "young men" not to enlist in the armed forces, declared that "the good soldier" never tried "to distinguish right from wrong," and if "ordered to fire down a crowded street when the poor was clamoring for bread, he obeys and sees the gray hairs of age stained with red and the life tide gushing from the breasts of women, feeling neither remorse nor sympathy. . . ." The article concluded:

> *No man can fall lower than a soldier—it is a depth beneath which he cannot go. Keep the boys out of the army. It is hell. Down with the army and the navy. We don't need killing institutions. We need life-giving institutions.*

The article, which was reprinted under London's name and widely distributed by the I.W.W., caused a furore. London, however, kept quiet until he discovered that the article was the cause of the withholding of his credentials. Then he publicly denied authorship of this "canard," and, in a letter dated August 5, 1916, stated that he had been denying responsibility for the article for years and argued that his books, newspaper reports, writings on prize-fighting and his war correspondence proved how ridiculous it was to accuse him of having written "The Good Soldier." "My opinion," he concluded, "is that it behooves a country or nation like the United States to maintain a reasonable preparedness for defense against any country or nation that at any time may go out upon the way of war to carve earth space for itself out of weaker and unprepared nations."

Whether or not Jack London actually wrote "The Good Soldier" will never be known since other articles were published in his name which he did not write. Yet it is difficult to believe that the *International Socialist Review* would have published the article under his name unless they had reasonable assurance that it expressed London's sentiments; nor did he protest the publication when it appeared. Again, parts of the article are reminiscent of his descriptions of the guards at the coronation of King Edward in *The People of the Abyss:* "Myriads of men, splendid men, the pick of the people, whose sole function in life is to blindly obey, and blindly to kill and destroy and stamp out life."

By the time London got to Mexico there was no war to report. After the Marines had landed and occupied Vera Cruz, the United States accepted the intervention of the ABC Powers—Argentina, Brazil and Chile. The Huerta government made its apologies, the American flag was saluted, reparations were promised and the threatened war was over before it had actually started. London was reduced to writing human interest articles which are important only in revealing how far he had travelled in his attitude towards the Mexican Revolution since 1911 and as further examples of his race chauvinism. Describing a meeting between a Mexican Lieutenant and an American Lieutenant, London wrote: "The Mexican Lieutenant strove to add inches to himself by standing on top of a steel rail. But in vain. The American still towered above him. The American was—well, American." In another article, he concluded: "To paraphrase Kipling the consistency of these half-breeds is to know no consistency."

Something of the socialist left in him kept asking whether it was not ridiculous to solve international problems by warfare, and he admitted that "War is a silly thing for a rational, civilized man to contemplate." But he justified American intervention with the comment that rational men could not be expected to settle problems in a rational way when others insisted on doing it "by violent means." Then he asked: "But in the meantime—and there you are—what would have been the present situation if the United States had long since disarmed? Somehow, I, for one, cannot see the picture of Huerta listening to and accepting the high ethical advice of the United States."

London saw nothing in the Mexican Revolution other than the universal desire to rob, pillage and loot, and to "shake down" the American oil interests "who had found and developed the oil-fields." It was America's duty, he argued, to save Mexico from "the insignificant portion of half-breeds who are causing all the trouble." Why bother to justify American armed intervention because "of a failure in formal courtesy about a flag?" London got down to brass tacks:

> *The exotic civilization introduced by America and Europe is being destroyed by a handful of rulers who do not know how to rule, who have never successfully ruled, and whose orgies at ruling have been and are similar to those indulged in by*

> *drunken miners sowing the floors of barrooms with the un-*
> *fortunate gold dust.*
>
> *The big brother can police, organize, and manage Mexico.*
> *The so-called leaders of Mexico cannot. And the lives and hap-*
> *piness of a few million peons as well as the many millions yet*
> *to be born, are at stake.*
>
> *The policeman stops a man from beating his wife. The*
> *humane officer stops a man from beating his horse. May not a*
> *powerful and self-alleged enlightened nation stop a handful of*
> *inefficient and incapable rulers from making a shambles and*
> *a desert of a fair land wherein are all the natural resources for*
> *a high and happy civilization?*

Granting even that London sincerely believed that American intervention would be of immeasurable benefit to the Mexican people and
that they would be happier and economically better off as an American
territory, how could one who had indicted the capitalists for mismanagement and for causing misery and poverty for their own people
believe that these same capitalists would institute an era of plenty for
the Mexican people? Certainly Jack London knew that even as he
wrote the economy of Mexico was largely in the hands of American
capitalists who used their control to keep the Mexican masses poverty-
stricken. Who, after all, had owned the factories of Rio Blanco which
he had described in "The Mexican," and who had been responsible
for the slaughter of the workers in these factories when they had gone
on strike?

Unlike Jack London, the American Socialist Party had not changed
its attitude towards the Mexican Revolution. On April 16, 1914, the
very same day that *Collier's Weekly* had wired London asking him to
cover the war in Mexico, the *New York Call,* the official organ of the
Socialist Party of New York, declared: "In spite of commercial
interests and all this honorable piffle (about the honor of the nation),
this war need not occur. President Wilson, tied down to the ideals of
his class, may not be able to stop it. But the American working class
can stop it." The day after the Marines landed at Vera Cruz, the
National Executive Committee of the Socialist Party wired President
Wilson denouncing the intervention. "The workers of the United
States have no quarrel with the workers of Mexico," the telegram asserted. And in *The Masses,* a leading Socialist magazine, John Reed,
who had spent four months with Pancho Villa's army in Mexico, cried

out that intervention would destroy the gains of the Mexican Revolution and called upon the people to oppose the war.

Jack London's Mexican articles aroused a storm of fury in the radical press all over the country. Even the liberal *Nation* expressed amazement. "That an eminent apostle of red revolution," it observed, "should audibly be licking his chops over millions of gold dollars wrested from its rightful owner, the Mexican peon, by the predatory ministers of international capital, is somewhat disconcerting." John Kenneth Turner, a leading socialist, bluntly charged in the *Appeal to Reason* that London had been bribed by the "flattering good fellowship" of the oil interests to turn out "a brief for the oil man, a brief for intervention, a brief for what Mexicans call 'Yankee Imperialism.'"

Upton Sinclair was a good deal kinder. A year after London's death, he recalled the series of articles from Mexico which had caused radicals "to turn from him in rage." But, Sinclair was convinced, these articles in *Collier's Weekly* did not signify that London had fallen away from socialism. Rather they meant that he had fallen "under the spell of the efficiency of oil engineers." "But I felt certain," Sinclair added, "that the exponent of capitalist efficiency who counted upon Jack London's backing was a child playing in a dynamite factory . . ." Unfortunately, the articles themselves hardly bear out this interpretation. At the same time, it is not necessary to subscribe to John Kenneth Turner's analysis of the motives behind London's articles. Jack London had not been won over by the good fellowship of the oil men. Nor had he been subsidized by them to write this material. His own way of life had produced the change. He had lost contact with the people; he had grown wealthy, had forgotten his lessons in socialism and his own lectures and essays on imperialism; and, as a tired and confused man, no longer bothered to look beneath the surface for basic causes. Perhaps his daughter, Joan London, analyzed it best when she wrote: "His was a more tragic sellout, for he had been subsidized, bought body and soul, by the kind of life he had thought he wanted, and it was destroying him."

Jack London returned from Mexico in the summer of 1914 a sick man, physically and mentally. He was weary and disillusioned and constantly searching for a haven where he could get away from it all and just rest. His land now came to mean everything to him, for he was turning away more and more from the activities that had once buoyed

up his spirits and had "handcuffed" him to life. "I am weary of everything," he told a reporter for the *Western Comrade,* a small socialist
paper. "I no longer think of the world or the movement (the social
revolution) or of writing as an art. I am a great dreamer, but I dream
of my ranch, of my wife. I dream of beautiful horses and fine soil in
Sonoma County. And I write for no other purpose than to add to the
beauty that now belongs to me. I write a book for no other reason
than to add three or four hundred acres to my magnificent estate. I
write a story with no other purpose than to buy a stallion. To me, my
cattle are far more interesting than my profession. My friends don't
believe me when I say this, but I am absolutely sincere." When the reporter asked him what he intended to do, London replied: "I feel
that I have done my part. Socialism has cost me hundreds of thousands
of dollars. When the time comes I'm going to stay right on my ranch
at Glen Ellen and let the revolution go to blazes. I've done my part."
Then as an afterthought, he added: "That's the way I feel now. I
suppose when the time comes I'll let my emotions get the best of my
intellect and I'll come down from the mountain top and join the fray."

But Jack London stayed on the "mountain top" until his death. In
February, 1915, hoping that the sun would cure his illness, he and
Charmian sailed for Hawaii. They spent severable enjoyable months
there and Jack's health improved. London took time off from his
writing to mingle with the "smart set." The business and social crowd
in Honolulu lionized him. In return, he spoke appreciatively of their
charities for the natives, a practice he had hitherto always condemned
in his socialist writings. Again he was roundly criticized by socialists
and liberals in the United States.

It was while in Hawaii that Jack London produced his final piece of
socialist writing, the introduction to Upton Sinclair's anthology, *The
Cry for Justice.* Sinclair had sent him the manuscript of his collection
of excerpts on social justice and asked London to write a foreword to
the volume. London replied promptly. The introduction, dated at
Honolulu, March 6, 1915, is one of the most moving and poetic
pieces to come from London's pen. Sinclair considered it "one of the
finest things he ever did," and believed that some paragraphs from the
introduction "might be carved upon his monument." London saw this
anthology of writings dealing with the struggle of the common people
for freedom throughout the ages as a Bible for the working-class which
would inspire understanding and sympathy and which, in turn, would
invariably lead to service in the cause of humanity. London wrote:

He, who by understanding becomes converted to the gospel of service, will serve truth to confute liars and make of them truth-tellers; will serve kindness so that brutality will perish; will serve beauty to the erasement of all that is not beautiful. And he who is strong will serve the weak that they may become strong. He will devote his strength, not to the debasement and defilement of his weaker fellows, but to the making of opportunity for them to make themselves into men rather than into slaves and beasts.

It is so simple a remedy, merely service. Not one ignoble thought or act is demanded of any one of all men and women in the world to make fair the world. The call is for nobility of thinking, nobility of doing. The call is for service, and, such is the wholesomeness of it, he who serves all, best serves himself.

We can agree with Upton Sinclair that "such words and actions based upon them make precious his memory and will preserve it as long as anything in American literature is preserved." For these lines of Jack London, written at a time when he was a sick and weary man, bring us the essence of the man and the message of his life. Despite his many shortcomings, he did serve justice and the working class faithfully in accordance with his lights. When one least expected it, there would come from his pen such an eloquent utterance as to cause one to forgive him his vacillations and his weaknesses. Such an utterance is the introduction to Sinclair's *The Cry for Justice*, and of a piece with it is the moving letter he wrote a few years before his death to the Central Labor Council of Alameda County:

I cannot express to you how deeply I regret my inability to be with you this day. But, believe me, I am with you in the brotherhood of the spirit, as all you boys, in a similar brotherhood of the spirit, are with our laundry girls in Troy, New York.

Is this not a spectacle for gods and men?—the workmen of Alameda County sending a share of their hard-earned wages three thousand miles across the continent to help the need of a lot of striking laundry girls in Troy!

And right here I wish to point out something that you all know, but something that is so great it cannot be pointed out

too often, and that grows every time that it is pointed out,—
AND THAT IS, THE STRENGTH OF ORGANIZED
LABOR LIES IN ITS BROTHERHOOD. There is no
brotherhood in unorganized labor, no standing together
shoulder to shoulder, and as a result unorganized labor is as
weak as water.

And not only does brotherhood give organized labor more
fighting strength but it gives it, as well, the strength of right-
eousness. The holiest reason that men can find for drawing to-
gether into any kind of organization is BROTHERHOOD.
And in the end nothing can triumph against such an organi-
zation. Let the church tell you that servants should obey their
masters. This is what the church told the striking laundry girls
of Troy. Stronger than this mandate is brotherhood, and the
girls of Troy found out when the boys of California shared
their wages with them. (Ah, these girls of Troy! Twenty weeks
on strike and not a single desertion from their ranks! And ah,
these boys of California, stretching out to them, across a con-
tinent the helping hand of brotherhood!)

And so I say, against such spirit of brotherhood, all machina-
tions of the men-of-graft-and-grab-and-the-dollar are futile.
Strength lies in comradeship and brotherhood, not in a throat-
cutting struggle where every man's hand is against man. This
comradeship and brotherhood is yours. I cannot wish you good
luck and hope that your strength will grow in the future, be-
cause brotherhood and the comrade-world are bound to grow.
The growth cannot be stopped. So I can only congratulate you
boys upon the fact that this is so.

Yours in the brotherhood of man,
Jack London.

Who, after all, but Jack London at those times when he forgot his
fetish about Anglo-Saxon supremacy could write so warm and human
a tribute to the plain working people of our country? One can certainly agree with Upton Sinclair when he wrote: "It was a fact that
you could never give Jack London up; he had a mind, a terrific mind,
which worked unceasingly, and impelled him irresistibly; he had a
love of truth that was a passion, a hatred of injustice that burned
volcanic fires."

Back in California, London threw himself into work, and between February and April, 1916, two books came off the press—*The Acorn-Planter*, his third play, and *The Little Lady of the Big House*, a novel carrying forward the back-to-the-land idea which London had advanced in *The Valley of the Moon* as the solution for the problems of modern industrial society. Neither of these books added to London's stature as a writer. They were written, it must be remembered, by a man who had soured on everything and everyone, and to whom the very act of writing was a nightmare. "You may think that I am not telling the truth," he told Emanuel Julius of the *Western Comrade*, "but I hate my profession. I detest the profession I have chosen. I hate it, I tell you, I hate it!" He continued in the same vein:

> *I assure you that I do not write because I love the game. I loathe it. I cannot find words to express my disgust. The only reason I write is because I am well paid for my labor—that's what I call it—labor. I get lots of money for my books and stories. I tell you I would be glad to dig ditches for twice as many hours as I devote to writing if only I could get as much money. To me, writing is an easy way to make a fine living. Unless I meant it, I wouldn't think of saying a thing like this, for I am speaking for publication. I am sincere when I say that my profession sickens me. Every story that I write is for the money that will come to me. I always write what the editors want, not what I'd like to write. I grind out what the capitalist editors want, and the editors buy what the business and editorial departments permit. The editors are not interested in the truth. . . .*

Once there had been a time when he could drop his hack-work and turn out an essay or story for *The Comrade, Wilshire's Magazine* or the *International Socialist Review*, and feel invigorated by the thought that thousands of workers would be reading his material and soapbox orators would be using it in their speeches. But now he was too sick, too tired to care. More and more he needed the stimulation of whiskey to make life bearable.

But John Barleycorn was beginning to take its toll. His uremia became worse. Once again he hoped that the Hawaiian sun would effect a cure. In January, 1916, he sailed for Honolulu. Sitting in his state-room he dictated his resignation from the Socialist Party to Charmian. Perhaps he knew that he was signing his death-warrant, for he did not forward it immediately. Then, after debating with himself whether to mail it or not, he decided to cut himself off completely from the Cause which had been so dear to him for more than twenty years, and sent the letter of resignation to the Oakland local:

Honolulu, March 7, 1916.

Glen Ellen
Sonoma County, California
Dear Comrades:

I am resigning from the Socialist Party, because of its lack of fire and fight, and its loss of emphasis upon the class struggle.

I was originally a member of the old revolutionary up-on-its-hind-legs, a fighting, Socialist Labor Party. Since then, and the present time, I have been a fighting member of the Socialist Party. My fighting record in the Cause is not, even at this late date, already entirely forgotten. Trained in the class struggle, as taught and practised by the Socialist Labor Party, my own highest judgment concurring, I believed that the working class, by fighting, by never fusing, by never making terms with the enemy, could emancipate itself. Since the whole trend of Socialism in the United States during recent years has been one of peaceableness and compromise, I find that my mind refuses further sanction of my remaining a party member. Hence, my resignation.

Please include my comrade wife, Charmian K. London's resignation with mine.

My final word is that liberty, freedom and independence are royal things that cannot be presented to nor thrust upon race or class. If races and classes cannot rise up and by their own strength of brain and brawn, wrest from the world liberty, freedom and independence, they never in time can come to these royal possessions . . . and if such royal things are kindly presented to them by superior individuals, on silver platters, they will not know what to do with them, will fail to make use of them, and will be what they have always been in the past . . . inferior races and inferior classes.

Yours for the Revolution,
Jack London.

No one in the Socialist Party was surprised by London's resignation; he had been drifting away from the movement ever since his return from the South Seas. Nonetheless, not a few socialists were annoyed that the man who had gone down to Mexico on a United States warship and then had written articles advocating American annexation of the land below the Rio Grande should decry the lack of revolutionary spirit in the Socialist Party. But those who questioned the sincerity of London's criticism of the Party overlooked the fact that however inconsistent he was in other respects as a socialist, London had never wavered in his insistence that socialist propaganda must be forthright and fearless and in his critical attitude towards the politicians in the leadership of the movement who were taking the Party along the road of expediency, opportunism and reformism. A year before he resigned, he told a reporter for the *Western Comrade* that he was deeply perturbed by the policy of compromise openly advocated by many Party leaders:

> *I became a Socialist when I was seventeen years old. I am still a Socialist, but not of the refined, quietistic school of socialism. The Socialists, the ghetto Socialists of the East, no longer believe in the strong, firm socialism of the early days. Mention confiscation in the ghetto of New York and the leaders will throw up their hands in holy terror. I still believe the Socialists should strive to eliminate the capitalist class and wipe away the private ownership of mines, mills, factories, railroads and other social needs.*
>
> *I do not believe that Socialists should soften and yield, eventually becoming mere reformers whose greatest desire is economy in government and low taxes, and the like. They should take upon themselves the task of doing away with the robbing capitalist system, do away with the profit system and place the workers in possession of the industries.*

London was among the earliest socialists, though not the only one, to perceive that reformism was steadily gaining ground among the leadership of the Socialist Party. In an article entitled "The Danger Ahead" published in the *International Socialist Review* of January, 1911, Eugene V. Debs had warned that the Party was in danger of becoming "permeated and corrupted with the spirit of bourgeois reform to an extent that will practically destroy its virility and efficiency as a revolutionary organization." On February 20, 1915, the *American*

Socialist featured an article which emphasized that the Party was becoming a "reformist political party . . . entirely lacking in class consciousness and revolutionary ideals. . . . Our party offices are being filled by men who appear to be far more solicitous for votes, political offices, and the good opinion of our enemies, than for the furtherance of those principles which make for the Revolution." And in April, 1916, one month after London's resignation, the *International Socialist Review* charged that the movement was dominated by middle class leaders "who spend precious time proving the post office and Panama Canal Socialist enterprises. From this type come suggestions that the class struggle, that impregnable fortress of the revolutionary workers, be dropped as obsolete because, presumably it is unpopular in the drawing rooms of the ultra respectable middle class. . . . To be brief, they would sugarcoat the pill so effectively that the masters might some day step down gracefully and fall in line!!! We are getting yards of this sort of thing in a supposedly Socialist press."

Instead of resigning, London could have thrown in his lot with the left-wing forces who shared his conviction that the Party had lost its militancy and joined them in seeking to check compromise tendencies and build a truly revolutionary movement. Yet the tragedy of London's position was that he no longer fitted anywhere in the movement. If his belief in revolutionary socialism made it impossible for him to work with the conservative socialists, his attitude towards the World War which had broken out in the summer of 1914 made it equally impossible for him, had he wished to do so, to cooperate with the left-wing socialists.

When the news of the European conflict reached the United States, socialists condemned it as an imperialist war and offered sympathy to their comrades across the ocean. On August 12, 1914, the National Executive Committee issued a manifesto extending the sympathy of the American Party "to the workers of Europe in their hour of trial, when they have been plunged into a bloody and senseless conflict by ambition-crazed monarchs, designing politicians and scheming capitalists. The workers have no quarrel with each other but rather with their ruling classes." Again, in December, 1914, the Committee proposed the Socialist Party Anti-War Manifesto which declared that while the immediate causes of the war were "thoughts of revenge . . . imperialism and commercial rivalries . . . secret intrigue . . . lack of democracy . . . vast systems of military and naval equip-

ment . . . jingo press . . . powerful armament interests," the fundamental cause was the capitalist system. This position was endorsed in
a referendum vote in September, 1915 by a large majority of the
membership.

This enraged Jack London. From the beginning of the war he had
announced his support of the Allies and had refused to accept the
position that it was a capitalist war. Germany was the "Mad Dog of
Europe"; the Allies had to be supported. If England was defeated, he
was prepared to go "into the last ditch" with her. The cause of the
war, as he saw it, was simple: "I believe that the present war is being
fought out to determine whether or not men in the future may continue in a civilized way to depend upon the word, the pledge, the
agreement, and the contract." He brushed aside the fact that millions
would die in the course of the conflict: "As regards a few million terrible deaths, there is not so much of the terrible about a quantity of
deaths as there is about the quantity of deaths that occur in peace
times in all countries in the world, and that has occurred in war
times in the past." "Civilization," he wrote, "at the present time is
going through a Pentecostal cleansing that can only result in good for
humankind."

Soon enough other socialists in America were to echo London's sentiments and his call for the entrance of the United States into the war
on the Allied side. Ironically enough, they were precisely the forces
in the Socialist Party whom London had condemned for advocating a
policy of compromise and for their abandonment of a militant, revolutionary program. The left-wing socialists continued to insist that
the carnage in Europe was the result of rival imperialisms in quest of
markets for exploitation. However much they agreed with London's
criticism of reformist tendencies in the Socialist Party, they could
have little to do with one who took such a jingoistic attitude towards
the war.

The Socialist Party replied to London's letter of resignation in a
sharply-worded article entitled "How You Can Get Socialism" which
appeared in the *New York Call* of March 27, 1916:

> *The Socialist Party never spends much time in lamenting
> over those who occasionally quit its ranks, nor will it do so
> now. Mr. London's letter, unfortunately, is couched in such
> vague and general terms that no one can be sure what he means.
> London is a fighter. Good. For some reasons not stated, he*

realized his fighting record in the cause is a closed chapter. He has of late found the party too peaceable for his taste. He quits it and goes elsewhere to find a battlefield.

Doubtless this sounds odd to us and to most party members. Yet doubtless London is sincere. The reasons may be local or personal, or both. We don't know Glen Ellen, and we do know Jack London. The name of the place does sound rather too idyllic to harmonize with the author of The Sea Wolf *and* The Call of the Wild.

We can only assure him that, however tediously peaceable membership in Glen Ellen may be, the workingmen in mine and shop and factory who make up the rank and file of the Socialist Party are fighting—not always an exhilarating, romantic, spectacular fight—not always the sort of fight that makes good copy for the magazines or good films for the movies—but the steady, unflinching, uncomplaining, unboasting, shoulder to shoulder and inch-by-inch fight that uses the fighters up one by one and sends them to the soon-forgotten graves, but that gains ground for those who fill up the ranks as they fall, that undermines the enemy's defenses and wears him down and keeps on wearing him down until the time comes for breaking his line and making the grand dash that shall end the war.

Live long, Friend London, and keep the pugnacious spirit, that, when the way to victory has been prepared by the unheralded millions, you may be with us once more on that dramatic day. We shall go on doing our best to hasten it for you.

It was an angry reply, and it stung London. As the months passed he grew more embittered over the attacks against him for having deserted the Cause. He was convinced that in a few years the Socialists "will have entirely forgotten that a fellow named Jack London ever did a stroke to help along." A few months after his resignation he wrote bitterly: ". . . because the socialists and I disagreed about opportunism, ghetto politics, class consciousness, political slates, and party machines, they too, have dismissed all memory, not merely of my years of fight in the cause, but of me as a social man, as a comrade of men, as a fellow they ever embraced for having at various times written or said things they described as doughty blows for the Cause. On the contrary, by their only printed utterances I have seen, they deny I ever struck a blow or did anything for the Cause, at the same time affirming that all the time they knew me for what I was—a Dreamer."

His discouragement was intense. Without the movement he drifted aimlessly. Like Martin Eden he now had no reason to continue living.

During all these months, as if by habit, he was writing stories that he would never see in print and most of which it would have been better to have destroyed. Six volumes of London's works were to appear after his death: * *The Human Drift,* unimportant sociological essays; *Jerry of the Islands* and *Michael, Brother of Jerry,* both inferior dog stories; *The Red One* and *On the Makaloa Mat,* collections of short stories not one of which is outstanding; and *Hearts of Three,* a movie story written for Hearst's *Cosmopolitan* for which he received $25,000 but which was never filmed.

Hawaii could no longer cure London. He returned to Glen Ellen, his body bloated with disease, pain-wracked and miserable. He was desperately lonely and made vain overtures for friendly relations with his former wife and his two daughters. His drinking, always excessive, reached new extremes. The inevitable end was drawing near.

On the morning of November 22, 1916, Jack London was found in a coma. The doctors ascribed his state to an overdose of morphine, deliberately taken. He never recovered, responding only once during the treatments and then relapsing into unconsciousness. At about seven in the morning he died. His ashes were buried on a hill on his ranch as he had directed his sister Eliza only two weeks before.

In the announcements to the press London's death was attributed to "a gastro-intestinal type of Uremia." But, as Upton Sinclair pointed out in a letter to R. W. Francis, September 21, 1932: "Several of Jack London's intimates knew that he had committed suicide." The manner of his death London had forecast years before: "Yet suicide, quick or slow, a sudden spill or a gradual oozing away through the years, is the price which John Barleycorn exacts. No friend of his ever escapes making the just, due payment." The prophecy he had made in *Martin Eden,* the final victory of the "white logic," was fulfilled.**

* The last book published before London's death was *Turtles of Tasman* which appeared in September, 1916. It was a collection of several stories and a play previously published in magazines.

** In February, 1914, the *Medical Review of Reviews* featured a "Sym-

The *New York Times'* obituary made no mention that he had ever been a socialist. A day later, in an editorial, the *Times* again omitted the word "socialism" but did remark that "he was at once happiest and least effective when the artist became the preacher." "By Jack London's death," the editorial concluded, "American letters suffer a heavy loss, as by his life they incurred a heavy debt."

The socialist journals carried more moving tributes. His inconsistencies were forgiven, his resignation from the Party was attributed to his state of health, and the main emphasis was placed upon the great contribution he had made through his writing and speeches, his never-failing generosity to the fund drives and his devotion to the working-class and its struggles. *The Masses* commented: "Jack London brought true science and the pulse of revolution for the first time into English fiction. . . ." *The Intercollegiate Socialist* observed: "In the untimely passing of our Comrade Jack London our Society has lost one of its pioneers, our first president, and for a long time our earnest friend and helper. . . . During his last years his efforts have mainly been directed to his literary work, but he was still young, and our Society might well have expected a renewal of his help in later years." In April, 1917 the *International Socialist Review* carried a tribute to Jack London which might well have been inscribed on the rock that stood over his ashes:

> *Our Jack is dead!*
> *He who arose from us*
> *And voiced our wrongs;*
> *Who sang our hopes,*
> *And bade us stand alone,*
> *Nor compromise, nor pause;*
> *Who bade us dare*
> *Reach out and take the world*
> *In our strong hands.*
> *Comrade! Friend!*
> *Who let the sunshine in*
> *Upon dark places.*
> *Great ones may not understand,*

---

posium on Euthanasia." Jack London's contribution went: "Man possesses but one freedom, namely the anticipating the day of his death. Should collective man (the state) rob individual man of this one freedom? I believe not. I believe in the individual's right to cease to live. . . ."

Nor grant you now
The measure of your mede;
But, in the days to come,
All men shall see.
Father of Martin Eden
And the Iron Heel—
Yes, men shall know
When we arise
And fight to victory!

Jack London was only 40 when he died, and he began publishing at the start of the century; yet in those 16 years he wrote nineteen complete novels, eighteen books of compiled short stories and articles (152 in all), three plays and eight books autobiographical and sociological. He wrote too much, and in the end too hurriedly. If he wanted a fine saddle horse or a yawl, a story purchased it. Caught up in a system which offered huge rewards for a writer with a name, yet hating this system for the misery it produced for so many people, he ended up in a mass of confusion and contradiction. With the waning of his socialist activity and his drift away from the working class and working class ideas in his last years, Jack London lost the inspiration and the ability to write valid literature. But in spite of all this, he remains one of America's most significant writers because he concerned himself with the vital problems of his age. Of working class origin, he was the first American writer to portray his class sympathetically and one of the few to use literature for building the foundations of a future society. He was not educated in a formal sense, but his comprehension was so great that he rose above educated men in ability and power to portray in his writings the fundamental issues of our times. The spirit of the common people of America, heroic, fiery and adventurous, will live forever in the pages of his rebel stories, novels and essays.

Supplementary Material

Page 24, line 4:

Jack London later illustrated how important it was to have English-speaking lecturers in the Socialist movement. "I remember," he told an interviewer in 1912, "that in Oakland, for example, it was a couple of little Russian Jews who first organized our local and started the free speech scrap up in Washington. They got up to their little soap boxes in Spokane and fairly jumped out of their skins trying to get themselves arrested in the cause of free speech. But in a few days they came to us with tears in their eyes, and said that the people were paying no attention to them. The Spokaners had told them to learn to speak English before they undertook to teach them anything. . . ." (*New York Call,* January 28, 1912.) London, however, paid tribute in the same interview to these Jewish Socialists, observing that it "was the same little, narrow-chested foreign Comrades who started the whole shooting match in the way of Socialism in our parts."

Page 27, line 18:

London's debut as a street speaker for the Socialist cause took place on February 12, 1897. He was arrested and jailed, but acquitted with a warning.

Page 48, line 26:

Russell Ames, in his unpublished study of Jack London as a social critic, believes that the Kempton-Wace letters have a greater importance than I have indicated. He points out that "London's insistence that reproduction was woman's peculiar function and nutrition man's, and his claim that women cannot reason about love, do not make up a major part of the book." As he sees it, the important part of the book is the picture London gives "of the primary creative and revolutionary role in history of the 'doer,' the scientist and technician, as opposed to the artist subservient to the demands made by the ruling classes." While I would agree with this point, I still believe that the Kempton-Wace letters truly reflect London's backward ideas on women.

Page 52, line 4:

The flyleaf of a copy of *The People of the Abyss,* in the possession of Mr. Ray Evans of Toronto, Canada, has the following inscription:

"My Dear Geneva Boggs

"Walk with me here & find a few more reasons why I am a Socialist.

> "Sincerely yours,
> "Jack London
> "Glen Ellen, Calif., Oct. 12, 1911."

Page 58, line 4:

There is increasing doubt among Jack London scholars as to the authenticity of this piece. During his lifetime, articles were often attributed to Jack London which he denied writing. The problem with establishing the authenticity of the description of a scab is that it appears to have been published after his death and no evidence thus far has appeared which establishes it as having been published during his lifetime. Hensley C. Woodbridge of Murray State College of Murray, Kentucky, who is preparing a bibliography of all of Jack London's writings, wrote to me on December 21, 1962: "Of course, at the moment, I am most doubtful as to the authenticity of the scab piece and will continue to be until I can discover some printings over his name during his lifetime. . . . In sum, if it were published during his lifetime and not disowned by him, I would be glad to call it his; otherwise there is no alternative but to call it spurious."

Labor papers have frequently published the scab definition and attributed it to Jack London, but thus far no labor paper published during London's lifetime has been found which carried the definition.

There is, however, significant internal evidence that the piece was written by London. He was fond of using Judas Iscariot as a symbol of the traitor. Indeed, the language used in the definition of the scab and that used by London in his definition of "the pot of money" in his article "Something Rotten in Idaho" is almost identical. (*See below*, pp. 134–35.)

Page 59, line 13:

In fairness to London, it must be noted that the "Yellow Peril," as he saw it, was not the usual nonsense about the danger of great waves of people of different color entering our land to sully white "purity." In his essay "The Yellow Peril" (1904), London asks if the Japanese religion may not be as great a religion as Christianity, and he concedes that any great race adventure "must have behind it an ethical impulse, a sincerely conceived righteousness." Then he adds: "But it must be taken into consideration that the above postulate is itself a product of Western race-egotism, urged by our belief in our own righteousness and fostered by a faith in ourselves which may be as erroneous as are most fond race fancies." Only London's questioning of the correctness of "fond race fancies" makes it possible to believe that the same man wrote in "Revolution" (1908):

"The comradeship of the revolutionists is alive and warm. It passes over geographical lines, transcends race prejudice, and has even proved itself mightier than the Fourth of July, spread-eagle Americanism of our forefathers. The French socialist workingmen and the German socialist workingmen forget Alsace and Lorraine, and, when war threatens, pass resolutions declaring that as workingmen and comrades they have no quarrel with each other. Only the other day, when Japan and Russia sprang at each other's throats, the revolutionists of Japan addressed the following message to the revolutionists of Russia: 'Dear Comrades— Your government and ours have recently plunged into war to carry out their imperialistic tendencies, but for us socialists there are no boundaries, race, country, or nationality. . . .'"

Page 70, line 16:

Of the sponsors, only Leonard D. Abbott, Jack London, and Upton Sinclair were members of the Socialist Party at that time.

Page 70, line 36:

Many of the sponsoring organizations billed London as "Daring Traveler," "An Original Klondiker," "Experienced Seaman," and "The American Kipling." Radical groups, however, billed him as "Prominent Socialist" and "Novelist and Socialist Friend of the Underdog."

Page 71, line 33:

London spoke at New York's Grand Central Palace on January 19, 1906. Before he spoke, hawkers sold ten-cent red flags described as "genuine, blood-red, Jack London souvenirs of a great and momentous occasion." The *New York Times* announced the following day: "They All Wear Red to Hear Jack London."

Page 76, line 21:

This had already been made clear during London's Grand Central Palace speech in New York on January 19, which a *New York Times* reporter had covered. During his speech, London had suggested that the workers might be forced to say, "To hell with the Constitution." He was interrupted by an old soldier in the audience who asked if the speaker were quoting someone or expressing an opinion. London answered that he was quoting a soldier who had used the remark in justifying the unconstitutional imprisonment of striking miners in Colorado by the militia. "Mother" Mary Jones, the veteran labor organizer, who had herself been frequently imprisoned during strikes, leaned out from her honored position in one of the boxes to shout, "Yes, and it was a general." All this was reported the next day in the *New York Times,* which also mentioned that as London continued the address, the old soldier stalked from the hall "with his head high."

Actually, it was not Adjutant General Brigadier General Sherman M. Bell, commander of the Colorado Militia, who made the remark, as "Mother" Jones and Upton Sinclair stated, but Judge Advocate Major Thomas McClelland. In her *Autobiography,* published twenty years later, "Mother" Jones corrected the remark about General Bell and charged McClelland with it. (Chicago, 1925, pp. 107–08.)

Page 86, line 24:

London defined "the pot of money" as follows:

"Why do some mine owners dislike Moyer, Haywood and Pettibone? Because these men stand between the mine owners and a pot of money. These men are leaders of organized labor. They plan and direct the efforts of the workingmen to get better wages and shorter hours. The operation of their mills will be more expensive. The higher the running expenses, the smaller the profits. If the mine owners could disrupt the Western Federation of Miners, they would increase the hours of labor, lower wages, and thereby gain millions of dollars. This is the pot of money.

"It is a fairly respectable pot of money. Judas betrayed Christ to crucifixion for thirty pieces of silver. Human nature has not changed since that day, and it is conceivable that Moyer, Haywood and Pettibone may be hanged for the sake of a few millions of dollars. Not that the mine owners have anything personally against Moyer, Haywood and Pettibone (Judas had nothing against Christ), but because the mine owners want the pot of money. Judas wanted the thirty pieces of silver."

Page 87, line 22:

Ghent's book grew out of an article he had written for the *Independent,* "The Next Step: A Benevolent Feudalism." Published on April 6, 1902, it aroused such widespread discussion that Ghent decided to expand it into a book.

Page 87, line 24:

"The future society that Ghent pictured," writes Harold Sherburn Smith, ". . . was not the pleasant land of equality and harmony portrayed in [Edward Bellamy's] *Looking Backward* or in William Dean Howells' *A Traveller from Altruria,* the best known of the recent utopian works. A spirit of sardonic pessimism suffused Ghent's description of a reborn feudalism. He professed to see peace in the society of the future, but it was a regimented peace, the peace of the modern police state, of fascism." ("William James Ghent, Reformer and Historian," unpublished Ph.D. thesis, University of Wisconsin, 1957, pp. 82–83.)

Page 87, line 29:

London's review appeared in the May, 1903, issue of the *International Socialist Review* (vol. IX, pp. 648–52) under the heading "Contradictory Teachers." This was a reference to the two books which were reviewed: Ghent's *Our Benevolent Feudalism* and John

Graham Brooks' *The Social Unrest*. London felt that the "two books should be read together." Ghent, whom he describes as "sympathetic to the Socialist movement," followed "with cynic fear every aggressive act of the capitalist class." Brooks, who "yearns for the perpetuation of the capitalist system as long as possible," viewed with "grave dismay each aggressive act of labor and Socialist organization." The two books thus represented "the two sides which go to make a struggle so great that even the French Revolution is insignificant beside it; for this latter struggle, for the first time in the history of struggles, is not confined to any particular portion of the globe, but involves the whole of it."

London summarizes Ghent's view as follows: "The coming status which Mr. Ghent depicts, is a class domination by the capitalists. Labor will take its definite place as a dependent class, living in a condition of machine servitude fairly analogous to the land servitude of the middle ages. That is to say, labor will be bound to the machine, though less harshly, in a fashion somewhat similar to that in which the earlier serf was bound to the soil." He describes Ghent's arguments "as cunningly contrived and arrayed. They must be read to be appreciated."

In commenting on Brooks' *The Social Unrest*, London points out that the author reveals the existence in the United States "of an extreme and tyrannically benevolent feudalism very like to Mr. Ghent's. . . ." The example he cites in this connection demonstrates that this "feudalism" was "tyrannical," but the "benevolent" side of it is difficult to discern. Thus London advises his readers to "witness the following" from Brooks' work:

"I asked one of the largest employers of labor in the South if he feared the coming of the trade union. 'No,' he said, 'it is one good result of race prejudice that the negro will enable us in the long run to weaken the trade union so that it cannot harm us. We can keep wages down with the negro, and we can prevent too much organization.'

"It is in this spirit that the lower standards are to be used. If this purpose should succeed, it has but one issue—the immense strengthening of a plutocratic administration at the top, served by an army of high-salaried helpers, with an elite of skilled and well-paid workmen, but all resting on what would essentially be a serf class of low-paid labor and this mass kept in order by an increased use of military force."

In quoting the above from Brooks' *The Social Unrest*, London reveals an understanding that racial prejudice is a device of the employer class to keep the workers under domination. It is unfortunate that this understanding was lacking in so many of his writings.

Page 89, line 8:

Ghent predicted that under the new feudalism the masses, in exchange for liberty, would have security. Here is how Ghent described the approaching utopia:

"Gradually the various processes in the social life merge . . . into a definite and confined stream of tendency. A more perfect, a better coordinated unity develops in the baronial class, and the measure of its control is heightened and extended to a golden mean which insures supremacy with peace. The under-classes settle in their appointed grooves, and the professional intermediaries definitely and openly assume their dual function of advisers to the barons and of interpreters to the people of the baronial will and ways. Laws, customs, and arts, all the institutions and social forces, change with the industrial transformation, and attain a finer harmony with the actual facts of life." (*Our Benevolent Feudalism,* pp. 196–97.)

Ghent also predicted that the masses, "remembering the chaos, the turmoil, the insecurity of the past, will bless its reign" and remain supine under the new feudalism. However, London, in *The Iron Heel,* describes the organization of the movement, based on the discontent of the masses, to overthrow the Oligarchy. Even though the revolt is crushed, it is clear that London believes that the masses will eventually triumph.

Page 90, line 37:

Sam S. Baskett asserts that London derived the sections dealing with the role of the church in American capitalist society from material on this subject appearing in the *Socialist Voice* of Oakland, California. ("A Source of *The Iron Heel,*" *American Literature,* May, 1955, pp. 268–70.) Probably this is true, though much the same type of material was appearing in socialist newspapers and magazines all over the country. What is strange is Baskett's conclusion: "This dependence [on the *Socialist Voice*] should serve as further evidence that London was not deeply versed in the works of Karl Marx, that he either preferred or found it necessary to obtain much of his knowledge of socialism indirectly from secondary materials." (p. 270.) While it is true that London read little of Marx and Engels besides the *Communist Manifesto,* there would have been nothing strange, even if he had been steeped in *Das Kapital* and other works of Marx, in his using contemporary American socialist sources to describe the role of the clergy in American society.

Page 96, line 36:

London developed this theme in a number of interviews. On January 28, 1912, the *New York Call,* a Socialist daily, carried an interview with Jack London by Joseph Gollomb under the heading: "London Tells of Social Revolution. Scouts Idea That It Will Be Realized Without Force." The interview opened:

"Do you still think," I asked him, "in view of the big strides we are making, that there is going to be the big flare-up, the huge shindy that you speak of in your 'Iron Heel'?"

"I don't see how it can be avoided," he remarked placidly.

"But suppose we get, as we shall, a sweeping plurality of a thousand to one over the capitalists—"

"Why, bless it all—(only he did not say 'bless')*—why, bless it all, you don't suppose the caps are going to hand over peacefully their nice, fat holdings simply because we shall win on a legal technicality! (Shade of Marx! a technicality!) You don't for one moment suppose they will lie down simply because we count more noses than they! Not on your life! Not as long as $5 a day will buy whole regiments of trained killers like the Pennsylvania State Constabulary!"

"But there'll be a thousand to every handful of them!"

"And a lovely chance your untrained, unorganized thousands will have against a compact little group of these fellows with the lust and talent for killing in their hearts and the latest thing in machine guns in their hands!"

---

* Gollomb explained that Charmian London had asked him "not to publish what she called her husband's 'profanity.' " He added: "With deep regret, I shall not. But I must say with all deep respect for the fine sensibilities of women in general and Comrade Mrs. London in particular, there are some beauties to which they are not alive. To call Jack London's swearing 'profanity' is it iself almost profanity. For keep in mind that Comrade London is a literary artist and that joyous vitality is his dominant note. So that when he swears it gives fellowship, exuberance, emphasis to what he says, like the echo of the hunting horn, the clink of glasses to the toast, or the pistol-crack of a well-snapped whip. 'Profanity,' indeed."

"But do you think there will be enough of these to put up much of an argument?"

"Yes. And don't forget the army of dependents and parasites on the capitalist class who are attached to them and to the present order. Together they make up quite an item and will stick to their masters and fight for them, especially as their masters will make it worth their while to stay by them. Oh, never you fear . . . the Big Scrap is coming!"

"All right," I assented. "When?"

Comrade London laughed a disclaimer.

"I've quit prophesying dates for the social revolution. In high school I laid a lot of bets that it was due in ten years and felt sure of my money. Well I hope none of the fellows come around to collect."

"You don't think, then, that peaceful propaganda of reasoning education and conversion will do the trick?" I asked, to bring him back to his strenuous theme.

"Great Caesar" (or words to that effect). "No! I went through that stage when I believed in my salad days. I said to myself then: 'Now look here. Socialism is as plain as 2 plus 2 equates 4. All I need to do is to show the next fellow that and he'll tell the next fellow and in this way it will become 4 plus 4 equals 8, 8 plus 8 equals 16— and in just no time Socialism will be all over the shop, and come riding in on a flowing decked triumphal car.'

"There I saw the fellow whom I thought I had converted the day before was doing the same blessed thing and thinking the same as before I struck him. Furthermore, I saw while we were carrying on our little propaganda talk the capitalists were not losing time or ground themselves—not by a good deal. Why don't you know the caps are a good deal stronger today than they were ten years ago!

"Oh yes, I've changed my tune since those young days. I used to say of the caps and those who didn't come around to Socialism, 'We'll love them to it.' That's all behind me now. That's the only spirit in which to carry on our propaganda. Don't lose yourselves on a fog of talk, in oceans of hog-wash, softsoap and rose water. Get down to the brass tacks of the struggle. By all means get the ballot. But better still get the spirit. Get the good Western fighting spirit that gets up and shouts and keeps on shouting, 'Fight, damn you, fight!'"

Page 96, line 38:

Later, London added to this concept the idea that the capitalist use of force was teaching the workers to reply in kind, a policy of which he approved. He expressed this most clearly in an interview published in the *San Francisco Bulletin* of December 12, 1913, discussing the Wheatland Hop-Fields Riot, which occurred on August 3, 1913, on the Durst Brothers ranch in Wheatland, California. When the hop pickers, led by the I.W.W., revolted against abominable wages and working conditions, a posse, called in by the Dursts, attempted to disperse the striking hop pickers and arrest their leaders, especially Richard Ford and Herman Suhr. In the riot that followed the sheriff's firing a shot in the air, two county officials and two striking hop pickers were killed. Jack London, who met and interviewed many of the hop pickers after they fled in terror from the scene of the riot to escape arrest, was asked by a reporter for the *Bulletin* to explain the incident. The interview appeared under the heading: "Novelist Explains Hop Riots. Jack London Says Ruling Class Is Responsible for Workers' Use of Force." London explained:

"These men were not organized. There was only one among the 2,300 that held an I.W.W. card.* But they did not need organization. They have seen the cost of living go higher and higher, their purchasing power get less and less; they have all felt within themselves, 'Something has got to be done.'

"They have seen the aristocrats of labor, with their organizations become less oppressed than themselves, having greater purchasing power. They have heard the Socialists talking about the miraculous things to come through voting, but they themselves had no vote.**

"And, above all, they have had force preached to them, pounded into them, from the beginning—by whom? By the employers. By the Government. These things were in their mind when that Sheriff's automobile came rushing into their midst, and set fire to the powder.

"Of course, the employers have always ruled the working class with force. One incident happened that was strangely typical. One of

* Actually, there were about 100 I.W.W. card-carrying workers on the Durst ranch.

** London here was referring to the fact that the hop pickers were migratory workers who did not live in one area long enough to qualify for voting. Moreover, many were foreign-born, Japanese, Hindu, Cubans, Italians, Finns, etc., and were not yet naturalized citizens.

the Durst brothers struck one of the leading workmen over the face.* He said he did it 'facetiously.' Maybe he did; it isn't likely. But facetious or not, that blow symbolized the whole relation between employer and employe. Where they do not actually strike blows it is because the blows will be struck back.

"Now, the Sheriff and the District Attorney came on the scene, not at all in the interests of equity, but in the interests of the employer. They were not there to see fair play; they were there to 'keep order'; that is to say, to quell the hop pickers. The Sheriff expected his shot in the air to cow them."

"Why didn't it cow them?" was asked. "It would have done so a few years ago."

"Simply because they are becoming more and more imbued with the belief that force is the only way. I look back over history and I see that never has the ruling class relinquished a single one of its privileges except it was forced to. I do not understand wherein the ruling class today may have any different psychology from the ruling class at any other time in history."

"But," was asked, "does not your reading of history also teach you that the concessions gained by force have failed to stick?"

"No; I can see that the negro was given suffrage without his fighting for it; the masters got together and handed it down to them, and today he stands by, impassive and indifferent, while they take it away from him again.** It is always the things we fight for, bleed for, suffer for, that we care the most for.

---

* The man who was struck was Richard "Blackie" Ford. Ford and Suhr were tried for murder of District Attorney Manwell, and although it was conceded that neither had fired the fatal shot, they were found guilty of having incited the firing by their agitation to organize the hop pickers and lead them in the strike, and were sentenced to life imprisonment.

** London here revealed his total ignorance of the history of the Negro people in the United States. Not only did the Negroes fight for suffrage, before the Civil War, during the Civil War, in which over 200,000 served in the Union armed forces, and during the Reconstruction period, but they were anything but "impassive and indifferent" in 1913, when London issued this statement. The National Association for the Advancement of Colored People, organized by W. E. B. Du Bois and other Negro leaders and white sympathizers, was waging an active campaign for restoration of the right of suffrage, guaranteed to the Negro people under the Fifteenth Amendment, as well as for other demands as part of its campaign for full equality.

In this connection, the following comment by London on the Abolitionists is of some interest. It was written on August 4, 1902 while he was en route

"And this is just as true of the employers as it is of the men underneath. They have always preached to the workers in terms of force.
The lesson is soaking into the workers; that is all. That is why we
have hop-field riots, and that is why we are going to have more of
them."

Page 97, line 34:

During his interview with Joseph Gollomb, published in the
New York Call of January 28, 1912, London had been asked: "How
can you bear to leave the interesting times that are coming with the
growth of Socialism in Europe and America, and go for years in the
back yards of civilization in Asia and the South Seas?" London explained:

"Well, I love Socialism. But there is the other passion in me. The
sky, the sea, the hills, wilds—I just love them and I must have them.
So I go where I can get them.

"But don't get the notion that when I cruise around the South Seas
that I am letting up on Socialism. Not a bit. Why, I've made speeches
for Socialism in Honolulu, in Samoa, and in Tahiti. And say," he
smiled in reflection, "in Tahiti our Comrades tried to get for me what
would be the Great Central Palace in this city. But the authorities,
as soon as they learned that I was going to speak on Socialism, shut
the door. So the Comrades got the Folies-Bergères, a sort of gay
resort. Even then, the Chief of Police came around and wanted me
to promise that I'd cut a lot of things out of my speech. I balked at
that. Then they got a couple of fellows who knew English to stand
by and listen, and to let the police know when I had said something
that was against the law. But these fellows couldn't make head or

---

to England, as part of a series of comments on Orlando Smith's book,
Eternalism:

"Then the Abolitionists, who were few in numbers, were irrational and
immoral, but became rational and moral when a great many came to believe
as they believed. Always, you will notice, a few men have believed a thing
first, and then, perhaps, the many. For sometimes a few men have believed
an ascertainable truth and have died without convincing their generation.
And it is even possible, considering how utterly apart is your position and
mine, that the few in every generation may believe an ascertainable truth
which the many in every generation will not believe."

London's letter to Orlando Smith, of which the above is a part, makes four-
teen single-spaced typewritten pages. It has never been published. The original
is in the possession of U. Grant Roman of Fort Lauderdale, Florida who has
kindly given me permission to quote from the letter.

tail of what I said, even though they knew English, so everything went off all right.

"In Samoa I talked in a beer garden—they're Germans, you know —the audience drank beer and ate while I talked and they listened. Every now and then they'd send up a glass of beer for me. It was very pleasant. In one place the Comrades, after my talk, organized a local on the spot, and affiliated themselves with the French Socialist party.

"And above all, I write all the time. And no matter what I write, whether it be a novel or romance, I can't help putting Socialism into it. . . ."

Gollomb concluded the interview on the following note: "There was no doubt in my mind as I left him that Socialism is as much a part of Jack London as the breath in his lungs. And I feel sure that as long as he breathes he will go on spreading that good, virile spirit that makes him sign himself invariably, 'Yours for the Revolution, Jack London.' "

Page 104, line 6:

Early in 1909, London had taken issue with Reverend Charles Brown, who, in a sermon on *Martin Eden* on January 16, 1909, at Oakland, had charged that the hero of the novel had failed because, as a Socialist, he had "lacked faith in God," an obvious attack on the author of the novel. London replied the very next day:

"Since hearing the Rev. Charles Brown's sermon last night on *Martin Eden,* I can understand why for two thousand years the Church has been rent with dissension over the interpretation of the Scriptures. Mr. Brown gave last night a splendid sample of the churchman's capacity for misinterpretation.

"Mr. Brown interpreted *Martin Eden* as a man who failed because of lack of faith in God. I wrote *Martin Eden,* not as an autobiography, nor as a parable of what dire end awaits an unbeliever in God, but as an indictment of that pleasant, wild-beast struggle of individualism of which Mr. Brown is not among the least of protagonists.

"Contrary to Mr. Brown's misinterpretation last night, Martin Eden was not a Socialist. Mr. Brown, in order to effect a parallel with my own life, said that Martin Eden was a Socialist. On the contrary, I drew him a temperamental, and later on, an intellectual, individualist. So much so was he an individualist that he characterized Mr. Brown's kind of ethics as a ghetto-ethics and Mr. Brown's kind of individualism as half-baked Socialism. Martin Eden was a proper Individualist of the extreme Nietzschean type.

"Now to my parable, which I thought I had expounded lucidly in the pages of this novel. Being an Individualist, being unaware of the needs of others, of the whole human collective need, Martin Eden lived only for himself, fought only for himself, and if you please, died only for himself. He fought for entrance into the bourgeois circles where he expected to find refinement, culture, high-living and high-thinking. He won his way into those circles and was appalled by the colossal, unlovely mediocrity of the bourgeoisie. He fought for a woman he loved and had idealized. He found that love had tricked him and failed him, and that he had loved his idealization more than the woman herself. These were the things he had found life worth living in order to fight for. When they failed him, being a consistent Individualist, being unaware of the collective human need, there remained nothing for which to live and fight. And so he died.

"All this is so clearly stated in the pages of the book that I am compelled to quote the following, which occurs when Brissenden asks Martin to go down with him to the Sunday night meeting of the Socialists. Brissenden says to Martin:

" 'Outsiders are allowed five-minute speeches. Get up and spout. Tell them what you think about them and their ghetto-ethics. Slam Nietzsche into them and get walloped for your pains. Make a scrap of it. It will do them good. Discussion is what they want, and what you want, too. You see, I'd like to see you a Socialist before I am gone. It will give you a sanction for your existence. It is the one thing that will save you in the time of disappointment that is coming to you. You have health and much to live for, and you must be hand-cuffed to life somehow.' "

"I cannot comprehend how, after reading such lines, Mr. Brown conceives Martin Eden to be a Socialist, nor how Mr. Brown failed so lamentably in grasping the thesis I have expounded.

"Martin Eden failed and died, in my parable, not because of his lack of faith in God, but because of his lack of faith in man. Even Mr. Brown will agree that he cannot get to God except through man. Martin Eden failed because he did not get even to man. He got only as far as himself, and the rest of humanity did not count.

"Unfortunately, Mr. Brown's sermon was not on *Martin Eden,* but on Jack London, and Mr. Brown was woefully unacquainted with the subject. He said that I was Martin Eden. Let me point out the vital weakness of his parallel—Martin Eden killed himself. I am still alive.

"Why am I alive? Because of my faith in man, a faith which Martin Eden never achieved, and a faith which Mr. Brown evidently did not know appertained to his subject, namely, Jack London. Yet my faith is most readily accessible to all men; my books are in the Public Library. Mr. Brown should have read up on the subject before he expounded it. Let me here quote some of my faith. I take the following from *What Life Means to Me:*

" 'I look forward to a time when man shall progress upon something worthier and higher than his stomach, when there will be a finer incentive to impel men to action than the incentive of today, which is the incentive of the stomach. I retain my belief in the nobility and excellence of the human, I believe that spiritual sweetness and unselfishness will conquer the gross gluttony of today. And last of all, my faith is in the working class. As some Frenchman has said, 'The stairway of time is ever echoing with the wooden shoe going up, the polished boot descending.' ' "

"Again I quote my faith, this time from the preface of my *War of the Classes:*

" 'He must learn that Socialism deals with what is, not with what ought to be; and that the material with which it deals, is the clay of the common road, the warm human, fallible and frail, sordid and petty, absurd and contradictory, even grotesque, and yet, withal, shot through with flashes and glimmerings of something finer and God-like, with here and there sweetnesses of service and unselfishness, desires for goodness, for renunciation and sacrifice, and with conscience stern and awful, at times blazing imperious, demanding the right—the right, nothing more nor less than the right.'

"Jack London"

London's letter to Rev. Brown was published in the Seattle *Socialist* of June 18, 1910. He sent it to the editor with the following explanation: "Dear Comrade: In your issue of May 28, you have an aritcle entitle 'A Little Debate,' in which Comrade Armstrong holds that I am a Socialist, and in which L. Manley insists, from his reading of my book, *Martin Eden,* that I am not. Wherefore, I am impelled to send you the reply I made to Rev. Charles Brown, when he misinterpreted *Martin Eden.* Please return this letter. Yours for the Revolution, Jack London."

Page 111, line 39:

The term "Wobbly" was used, especially after 1913, as denoting a member of the Industrial Workers of the World (I.W.W.). Although Jack London was not a member of the I.W.W., he was on very good terms with the organization. He was listed as a contributing editor by the *Industrial Worker,* official organ of the I.W.W. published in Joliet, Illinois, as early as 1906, although there is no evidence in the files of the paper that he ever contributed an article. London expressed his sympathy with the I.W.W.'s belief in sabotage and syndicalism. "I have believed in them for twenty years," he told an interviewer in 1913. (*New York Call,* June 2, 1913.) Upon his death in 1916, the official I.W.W. journal referred to London as "Our literary comrade." (*Industrial Worker,* May 27, 1916.)

Page 112, line 1:

London had been invited to deliver a speech at a meeting in behalf of the Mexican Liberals and their American friends to be held in the Labor Temple in Los Angeles on February 5, 1911. In lieu of the speech, he sent this letter which first appeared in the February 10, 1911, issue of the *People's Paper,* a Socialist journal published in Los Angeles.

Page 113, line 7:

The Junta was organized by Flores Magón. Magón had been editor of *La Revolución,* the socialist-anarchist organ of the Liberal Party formed in Mexico by Camilio Arriago in 1900. Though firmly and unswervingly committed to anarchist objectives, Flores Magón built a broad radical-liberal following both in Mexico and in the United States. Magón was frequently imprisoned in Mexico and the United States as a "socialist agitator." Exiled from Mexico, Magón and other exiled Liberal Party members operated after 1910 from Los Angeles, where they resumed publication of *La Regeneración* in September.

After the Diaz dictatorship was overthrown, the *Magonistas,* as the followers of Magón were called, sought a more thoroughgoing revolution than that promised under Madero. Although Flores Magón himself did not himself cross into Mexico, under his leadership, Mexicans, I.W.W. members, and assorted soldiers of fortune, seldom reaching three hundred men in all, captured Mexicali, Algodones, Tecate, El Alamo, and Tijuana. Unable to obtain adequate munitions and reinforcements, the revolutionists fell back to Mexicali and Tijuana, and agents of Madero negotiated surrender of the Mexicali garrison. Before a similar surrender could be achieved in Tijuana, Celso Vega, the savage but slow-moving territorial governor of Ensenada, aided by 150 southern California Mexicans, recaptured that border town and drove the remnants of the regiment back into the United States.

Page 114, line 14:

The story is also, like the earlier Jack London story, "A Piece of Steak," and the later novelette, *The Abysmal Brute,* a brilliant exposé of the callousness and commercialism of the prize ring. Danny Ward's handlers, manager, and even the referee are all involved in the plot to make him lose. The referee counts fast when he is down, and breaks his clinches. When he is winning, an attempt is made to bribe him, and when this fails, they plan to make it look as if he has fouled his opponent.

London, incidentally drops his racism in this story, and seems even to go out of his way to state, while describing the fight, that Rivera is "more delicately coordinated, more finely nerved and strung than any of them"—the white Americans. The hero of this story is not an Anglo-Saxon, but a Mexican worker, the son of a revolutionary working man, who has memories of child labor, starvation, exploitation, lock-out, the shooting down of workers, and the finding of the corpses of his father and mother in the piles of dead.

Page 116, line 33:

"Whose Business to Live," a story probably written by London during the time he was doing the series for *Collier's Weekly,* is filled with the same contempt for the Mexicans who are described as "greasers," "ungrateful," "cowardly," and "stupid." The plot concerns the escape of several American men and women from maddened "mobs" of Mexicans who were, to London's annoyance, bitter because American sailors and marines landed at Vera Cruz and took control of the city. The story was published in his final book of stories, *Dutch Courage and Other Stories,* which appeared in 1922.

Page 122, line 6:

The Little Lady of the Big House is probably the worst novel London ever wrote, even worse, especially so far as it reveals his

148   JACK LONDON

racism, than *The Mutiny of the Elsinore,* published in 1914. Charmian London called the latter novel "a whacking good sea-story, true,
modern, beneath the romance and action a heartfelt protest against
the decayed condition of the American merchant marine." A truer
interpretation would be to say that "beneath the romance and action"
is London's growing contemptuous loathing for nearly all the "lower
class" characters in his books, his idealization of the blond white
man from the northern countries of Europe who is being crowded
out by the overwhelming weight of the Latin, the Slav, and other
Southern European races who were pouring into America. Only by
stamping out, under an iron heel, the rebellious masses who challenge the reign of the "superior" blond white man could the latter's
hold on leadership in society be preserved, and it is clear that London
is beginning to approve of such a program.

All this is developed to its fullest extent in *The Little Lady of the
Big House.* London here finds "very tenable" the hypothesis that
"the white-skinned, blue-eyed Aryan, born to government and command, ever leaving his primeval, overcast and foggy home, ever
commands and governs the rest of the world and ever perishes because of the two-white light he encounters." When the Mate, Mr.
Pike, "killer and slave-driver, it is true," "sprang first into the teeth
of danger so that his slaves might follow," Pathhurst, the hero of the
novel, felt "pride that my eyes were blue, like his; that my skin was
blond, like his; that my place was aft with him, and with the
Samurai in the high place of government and command. As for the
rest—the weaklings and the rejected, and the dark-pigmented things,
the half-castes, the mongrel-bloods, and the dregs of long-conquered
races—how could they count? My heels were iron as I gazed on them
in their peril and weakness. Lord! Lord! For ten thousand genera-
tions and centuries we had stamped upon their faces and enslaved
them to the toil of our will."

The low point in the novel comes when Pathurst comments after
one of the leaders of the mutiny, a New York City gangster curses
him: "As I listened I knew why the English had blown their muti-
nous Sepoys from the mouths of cannon in India long years ago."

There are, to be sure, a few redeeming features in the novel. Dick
Forrest, who is really Jack London, rebukes one of his intellectual
friends for having a Southern prejudice against Negroes, and admits
curiously enough in such a book, that the "average Hottentot, or
the average Melanesian, is pretty close to being on a par with the

average white man." But he goes on to claim that the whites produce a much heavier percentage of men who are above the average. He asserts further that the Hottentots have produced no great man, the "Hawaiian race" but one, the Negroes in the United States but two—Booker T. Washington and W. E. B. Du Bois.

Jacobs, the supreme representation of the workers, the beasts, is the embodiment of all that is ugly, a complete caricature of the superior workers London had described in his socialist essays. To be sure, London pays his respect to Jacobs by picturing him as fearless, but this is only in passing. Jacobs' philosophy is set forth in the following statement he makes to Pathurst:

"Yes, he was a Red and knew his Kropotkin, but he was no anarchist. On the other hand, political action was a blind alley leading to reformism and quietism. Political socialism had gone to pot, while industrial unionism was the logical culmination of Marxism. He was a direct actionist. The mass strike was the thing. Sabotage, not merely as a withdrawal of efficiency, but as a keen destruction of profits policy, was the weapon."

Probably this revealed London's admiration for the philosophy and tactics of the I.W.W., but the rest of the novel showed that he had little respect at this time for that organization's emphasis upon labor solidarity and bitter opposition to racism in all its forms.

As for the "Little Lady" herself, she reveals her viewpoint when she (Paula) tells Dick Forrest and Evan Graham that she must love them both because: "You are successes. Your muscles are blond-beast muscles, your vital organs are blond-beast organs. And from all this emanates your blond-beast philosophy. That's why you are brass tacks and preach realism, and practice realism, shouldering and shoving and walking over lesser and unluckier creatures who don't dare talk back. . . ."

Graham has lost all his capital in the stock market, and has only "an income of several thousand a year left." "But he doesn't whimper." "He's good stuff, old American stock, a *Yale* man." Dick Forrest owns mines in Mexico and he insists that the Mexicans are too stupid to develop them. He praises Diaz and sneers at the Revolution.

These are the heroine and heroes of London's novel. It almost seems as if London had set out to satirize everything he had written only a few years before.

One who reads *The Little Lady of the Big House* and is tempted to dismiss Jack London as a progressive force in American life and literature would do well to bear in mind the following excellent comment by Russell Ames:

"London was such a mixture of . . . socialist worker and bourgois individualist, so glaringly wrong in theories about so many things, that is easy for us to feel superior to him, rightly, and to think we cannot learn from him, wrongly.

"This is not to say that such terrible weaknesses as London's racism should be tolerated. The point is that his enemies and those who should be his friends should not be allowed to use his weaknesses as clubs against his strong and good qualities. No doubt some critics are anxious to prove that London was a bad, phony, insincere and stupid socialist precisely because he was such a good socialist.

"Though London was clearly more patronizing in his view of the workers as a political force than any socialist intellectual would be today, he was also closer to the workers than most of us are.

"Jack London accepted, off and on, many undemocratic ideas; he tended to overestimate the power of the rich and to underestimate the organized strength of the workers (in his time the socialist and labor groups were especially numerous and divided), but there is no real question as to which side he was on." (Unpublished manuscript on Jack London in possession of the author, Oaxaca, Mexico.)

Page 128, line 7:

One story which London never finished has recently been published, called *The Assassination Bureau, Ltd*. London had written 40,000 words of this novel—based on a story idea bought from Sinclair Lewis—when he died. The final 20,000 words are by Robert L. Fish, who completed the book from London's notes. The novel tells of a society for hired assassinations, headed by Ivan Dragomiloff, composed solely of high-minded operatives who will kill only for the benefit of society. Millionaire Socialist Winter Hall hires the society to assassinate its chief, after proving to Dragomiloff (who is also Sergius Constantine, father of Winter's bride to be) that society will benefit by his own death.

The novel contains flashes of London's indictment of capitalist society. There are jibes at social workers who, by operating day nurseries for the children of women workers, enable the employers "more thoroughly . . . to sweat the mothers." There is a portrait of two labor leaders who are in the pay of the employers and have sold out their members in a number of strikes. There is the professor who joins the Assassination Bureau after he was forced to resign from Burlington University because his "economic teachings offended the founder." There are descriptions of crooked stock manipulations by supposedly respectable capitalists. Essentially, however, *The Assassination Bureau, Ltd.* is a clever and lively suspense novel.

London had already used a somewhat similar theme in two previous pieces. One was "The Minions of Midas" (1901) which is discussed above (pp. 45–46.) In "Goliah" (1910) he described the establishment of Socialism by dictatorship, assassination, and other forms of violence. Here again London showed his lack of understanding of the basic tenets of Socialism, which rejected all terrorist, anarchistic, individualistic policies and worked for the broadest of peaceful mass activity, condoning force only in those situations in which self-defense is necessary and peaceful progress barred.

It is interesting, however, to note that in *The Assassination Bureau, Ltd.*, London makes it quite clear that the whole idea of using assassination to benefit society is fundamentally anti-social. Even in "Goliah," he develops the idea that it is not Goliah, the hero of the story, who, through the use of terror, determines the progress, the forms, the institutions of Socialism, but the whole working people themselves. Thus he wrote: "And the beauty of it is that the people of the United States have achieved all this for themselves. . . . The fear of death made those in the high places get out of the way, that was all, and gave the intelligence of man a chance to realize itself socially."

Bibliography

UNPUBLISHED STUDIES

AMES, RUSSELL. "The Writings of Jack London," unpublished manuscript in possession of author, Oaxaca, Mexico.

BASKETT, SAM S. "Jack London's Fiction: The Social Milieu," unpublished Ph.D. thesis, University of California, 1951.

FRAUENGLASS, ETTIE. "Jack London as a Socialist," unpublished M.A. thesis, New York University, 1939.

HOLLAND, ROBERT BELTON. "Jack London: His Thought and Art in Relation to His Time," unpublished Ph.D. thesis, University of Wisconsin, 1950.

POPE, MARGARET L. "Jack London: A Study in Twentieth Century Values," unpublished Ph.D. thesis, University of Wisconsin, 1935.

ROSE, LISLE ABBOTT. "A Descriptive Catalogue of Economic and Politico-Economic Fiction in the United States, 1902–1909," unpublished Ph.D. thesis, University of Chicago, 1935.

ROTHBERG, ABRAHAM. "The House that Jack Built: A Study of Jack London," unpublished Ph.D. thesis, Columbia University, 1952.

SMITH, HAROLD SHERBURN. "William James Ghent; Reformer and Historian," unpublished Ph.D. thesis, University of Wisconsin, 1957.

YOUNG, THOMAS DANIEL. "Jack London and the Era of Social Protest," unpublished Ph.D. thesis, Vanderbilt University, 1950.

BOOKS

BAMFORD, GEORGIA LORING. *The Mystery of Jack London*, Oakland, Calif., 1913.

BLAISDALE, LOWELL L. *The Desert Revolution: Baja California, 1911,* Madison, Wisconsin, 1962.

CALVERTON, V. F. *The Liberation of American Literature,* New York, 1932.

FREEMAN, JOSEPH. *An American Testament,* New York, 1936.

HAZARD, LUCY LOCKWOOD. *The Frontier in American Literature,* New York, 1927.

HICKS, GRANVILLE. *The Great Tradition,* New York, 1933.

KAZIN, ALFRED. *On Native Grounds,* New York, 1942.

KIPNIS, IRA. *The American Socialist Movement,* 1897–1912, New York, 1952.

LAIDLER, HARRY WELLINGTON. *Twenty Years of Social Pioneering,* New York, 1926.

LEWISOHN, LUDWIG. *Expression in America,* New York and London, 1932.

LONDON, CHARMIAN K. *The Book of Jack London,* 2 vols., New York, 1921.

LONDON, JOAN. *Jack London and His Times,* New York, 1939.

MADISON, CHARLES A. *Critics and Crusaders,* New York, 1947.

McDEVITT, WILLIAM. *Jack London as Poet and as Platform Man,* San Francisco, 1947.

PARRINGTON, VERNON LEWIS. *Main Currents in American Thought,* New York, 1922.

PATTEE, FRED LEWIS. *Side-Lights on American Literature,* New York, 1922.

PAYNE, EDWARD BIRON. *The Soul of Jack London,* London, 1926.

RIDEOUT, WALTER B. *The Radical Novel in the United States,* 1900–1954, Cambridge, Mass., 1956.

SINCLAIR, UPTON. *The Cry for Justice,* Pasadena, Calif., 1925.

SINCLAIR, UPTON. *Mommonart,* Pasadena, Calif., 1925.

SPILLER, ROBERT E. and others. *Literary History of the United States,* 2 vols., New York, 1948.

STONE, IRVING. *Jack London: Sailor on Horseback,* Garden City, New York, 1947.

ARTICLES

AMES, RUSSELL. "Jack London: American Radical," *Our Time,* 7: 254–55, July, 1948.

"Attempt to Place Jack London," *Current Literature,* 42: 513–14, May, 1907.

Baggs, Mae Lucy. "The Real Jack London in Hawaii," *Overland Monthly*, n.s., 69: 405–10, May, 1917.

Bailey, Millard. "Valley of the Moon Ranch," *Overland Monthly*, n.s., 69: 411–15, May, 1917.

"Barbarian in Jack London, The," *Literary Digest*, 45: 564, October 5, 1912.

Baskett, Sam S. "A Source of *The Iron Heel*," *American Literature*, 27: 268–70, May, 1955.

Baskett, Sam S. "Jack London on the Oakland Waterfront," *American Literature*, 27: 363–71, May, 1955.

Bland, Henry Meade. "Jack London, Traveler, Novelist and Social Reformer," *The Craftsman*, 9: 607–19, February, 1906.

Colbron, Grace Isabel. "Jack London, What He Was and What He Accomplished," *Bookman*, 44: 441–51, January, 1917.

Dargan, E. Preston. "Jack London in Chancery," *New Republic*, 10: 7–8, April 21, 1917.

Eames, Ninetta. "Jack London," *Overland Monthly*, 25: 417–25, May, 1900.

Friedland, L. S. "Jack London as Titan," *Dial*, 62: 49–51, January 25, 1917.

Glancy, Donald R. "Socialist With a Valet: Jack London's 'First, Last and Only' Lecture Tour," *Quarterly Journal of Speech*, 99: 30–39, February, 1963.

Gollomb, Joseph, "London Tells of Social Revolution," New York *Call*, January 28, 1912.

Grattan, C. Hartley. "Jack London," *Bookman*, 68: 667–71, February, 1929.

Houck, C. B. "Jack London's Philosophy of Life," *Overland Monthly*, n.s., 84: 103–04, April, 1926, 156–57, May, 1926.

Huffer, O. M. "Jack London: A Personal Sketch," *Living Age*, 292: 124–26, January 13, 1917.

"Jack London," *Literary Digest*, 53: 1537, December 9, 1916.

"Jack London as His Wife Charmain Knew Him," *Current Opinion*, 71: 645–48, November, 1920.

"Jack London, Farmer," *Literary Digest*, 46: 1195, May 24, 1913.

"Jack London—In Memoriam," *International Socialist Review*, 17: 624, April, 1917.

"Jack London's Place in American Literature," *The Nation*, 103: 502, November 30, 1916.

"Jack London's Resignation from the Socialist Party," *Overland Monthly*, n.s., 69: 446, May, 1917.

"Jack London's One Great Contribution to American Literature," *Current Opinion*, 62: 46–47, January, 1917.

JAMES GEORGE WHARTON. "A Study of Jack London in His Prime," *Overland Monthly*, n.s., 69: 361–99, May, 1917.

JULIUS, EMANUEL. "The Pessimism of Jack London," New York *Call*, June 2, 1913.

MILLS, GORDON. "Jack London's Quest for Salvation," *American Quarterly*, 7: 3–15, Spring, 1955.

LANE, ROSE WILDER. "Life and Jack London," *Sunset Magazine*, 39: 34–37, 62, January, 1918, 40: 32–33, 68, February, 1918.

"Our National Honor," New York *Call*, April 16, 1913, 6.

"Placing Jack London's Books Under the Ban," *Arena*, 35: 435, April, 1906.

RUSSAK, MARTIN. "Jack London, America's First Proletarian Writer," *New Masses*, January, 1929, 13.

SILVER, G. V. "Jack London's Women," *Overland Monthly*, n.s., 74: 24–28, July, 1919.

SINCLAIR, UPTON. "About Jack London," *The Masses*, 10: 17–20, November and December, 1917.

SOCIALIST PARTY NATIONAL EXECUTIVE COMMITTEE. "Socialist Party Protests to the President," New York *Call*, April 23, 1914, 1.

STILLMAN, LOUIS J. "Jack London, Super-Boy," *Sunset*, 38: 42, February, 1917.

UNTERMANN, ERNEST. "Jack London, wie ich ihn kannte," *Sozialistich Monatshefte*, Berlin, July, 1929, 602–13.

WALLING, ANNA STRUNSKY. "Memories of Jack London," *The Masses*, 9: 13–17, July, 1917.

WALCUTT, CHARLES CHILD. "Naturalism and the Superman in London's Novels," *Papers of the Michigan Academy of Science, Arts and Letters*, 1948, Part IV, 89–107.

WEINSTEIN, JAMES. "The Socialist Party: Its Roots and Strength, 1912–1919," *Studies on the Left*, 1: 5–27, Winter, 1960.

WOODWARD, ROBERT H. "Jack London's Code of Primitivism," *The Folio*, 18: 39–44, May, 1953.